DATE DUE

DEMCO 38-296

American Indian Lives

Catch Colt

Sidner J. Larson

University of Nebraska Press

Lincoln and London

R

The excerpt on page 151 is from an unnamed sonnet by John Donne.

The paper in this book meets the minimum requirements of American
National Standard for Information Sciences—Permanence of Paper for
Printed Library Materials,
ANSI Z39.48-1984.

Library of Congress Cataloging-in-Publication Data
Larson, Sidner J., 1949–
Catch colt / Sidner J. Larson.
    p.   cm.—(American Indian lives)
ISBN 0-8032-2908-9 (cloth : alk. paper)
1. Larson, Sidner J., 1949–   . 2. Atsina Indians—Biography.
3. Atsina Indians—Social life and customs.   4. Fort Belknap Indian
Reservation (Mont.)—Social life and customs.   5. Shelby (Mont.)—
Social life and customs.   I. Title.   II. Series.
E99.A87L374   1995   978.6'15—dc20   94-32267   CIP

James Smith O'Bryan, Maggie Shambo
O'Bryan, Elwood "Buck" Cole, Marguerite "Sis" Cole, Ruth
Burtch Jeanette, Agnes Brockie Adams, Neil Cole, Skip Cole, and
Wink Cole were especially in my thoughts as I wrote this book; it
is nearly as much their story as it is mine. This book is dedicated
to my grandmother, Maggie Shambo O'Bryan, of the Otter Robe
family, Black Lodge Clan, who claimed me as one of her own.

Contents

Catch Colt

Meadowhawk, Blackbird, Thorn, Bull Calf

The old junior high school sat in the middle of a bare gumbo lot that, in turn, sat in the middle of Shelby. The lot sloped up steeply to the west, topped by a sidewalk heaved and broken by extremes of temperature. The building itself was a classic midwestern square block schoolhouse, only bigger and more outpostlike than the ones out in the country.

My brother and I had come here to play last year, and he fell off the little shed by the wide front steps, right on his head, and it swelled up on one side. He laid around the rest of the afternoon, then bounced back up and was running around again by evening.

Gary was a tough little guy, and sweet, with a crewcut and holes in his socks.

Gary and I had our annual fall reunion over cereal until I flipped a Cheerio over his barricade of boxes and milk carton and he started to holler. I had returned from the ranch the night before to find nobody there, and I was so tired I went to bed and fell asleep before anyone got home. Mom and Dean had been out on the town, and they didn't stir as Gary and I got ourselves up, fought awhile, then wandered off for the first day of school.

Although my mother kept Gary with her summers and so he was not a part of reservation life, he and I were close. We rough-housed constantly, and during one of our marathon wrestling matches he broke through a heating grate in the floor and his legs were kicking around inside the Oil City Bar below.

After I hauled Gary back up through the hole, Harvey Nelson, who owned the bar and the apartment above it, put his hands on his hips and swiveled his head to peer up at us. He stuck out the top plate of his false teeth and said, "One boy's a good boy, two boys you got half a boy, and three boys you got no boy at all." He had three boys of his own.

It might have seemed as if all we did was fight, but we also looked after each other. I bought him his first car, and his second, then built him a third with money he sent from Vietnam. When he got out of the service he had a box of medals awarded for service as a helicopter door-gunner, including being shot down in action twice.

Right after his discharge we drove the car I built for him, a hot-rod GTO, and a Honda 450 motorcycle from Montana to southern Oregon. We ate fruit from the roadside stands in Washington and Oregon, drank cheap wine sold in grocery stores, and shat like geese.

I could tell Gary was troubled, by the cynical, almost hopeless way he talked sometimes. He spoke of how frightened he was by combat in the beginning, then of how he came to relish the power of the M-60 machine gun he wielded. His first year of service was the last year of the war, and when it was over his company stood down at Fort Carson, Colorado, for the remaining two years of their enlistment.

He said that after the intensity of Vietnam, loafing around the army post for two whole years was maddening. He told me that after a short while he longed to return to war, where he had enjoyed status and power. He said he hated returning to the ordinary world, where he was just another face. He reminded me of the character Abel from Scott Momaday's book *House Made of Dawn,* only he didn't have a Pueblo to go home to. Sure enough, about a year later, I got a call from a veteran's hospital in Colorado telling me he had been shot through the chest.

After all my brother had been through, it seemed crazy he would get shot when he got home. He recovered physically, but he had other wounds I don't think the doctors ever reached. His recovery was only patchwork and there didn't seem to be much anybody could do about it. We lived far apart by then, but even if we had been closer, I didn't have the words or concepts yet to do myself much good, let alone someone else.

I worried about Gary for a long time, but he has his own family now and a good job he has held for more than ten years. He divides the rest of his time between a killer vegetable garden and pursuing Steelhead in the Oregon rivers near his home. Each passing year widens the distance between us, though, and somehow, that doesn't seem right.

Chimes were playing as I jumped down the narrow wooden steps three at a time from my mother's apartment above the Oil City Bar. The air was still and bright, and the railroad switchyard across the street smelled like diesel and creosote. I crossed the tracks and walked up onto Main Street toward the chimes.

When I got to the Catholic church, the chimes playing over the loudspeakers up in the bell tower were very loud. Kids went to school there, but we didn't know them so it didn't matter. Nor did we know the strange language of the mass, or the nave and apse within, or the bright-colored silk clothing of the alcoholic priest, so they didn't matter either.

I crossed the street past St. William's and cut through the Meadowlark grade school playground. I could see some of my sixth-grade friends over by the junior high, so I walked over and hung out with them until the bell rang. We all gathered on the first-floor landing where Mr. McDermott, the principal, and a number of other teachers were explaining how things worked.

They explained about changing classes, announced who was in the A, B, and C sections, then directed each section to its first hour homerooms. As my section began to file into Mr. Hawbaker's room, McDermott grabbed me by the shoulder and took me aside. He was tall, with a short, naturally wavy pompadour and the crisp speech of a city slicker.

As I stood wide-eyed, McDermott explained that he had heard about me and that things, by God, were going to be different for me this year. In fact, he said, he was going to make damn sure I

4

got the idea real quick who ran things around there. I had been making a hand with the men at the ranch the day before, and it was jarring to suddenly be treated like a child again.

I didn't say anything, but that mean fuck you of the brain must have crept onto my features. "You're a real hard case, aren't you mister?" he said, enunciating clearly. "Well, I've got a little surprise for you," he said, turning to walk away.

So much was going on that I didn't think much more about it, and I couldn't imagine what he could do to me beyond the usual measures.

My mother refused to leave her family for my father, although she did leave a few years later to follow one of my uncles to Shelby, Montana. The family was large—like those often found among tribal people—strongly opinionated, and successful within its own circumstances.

Moreover, the family was made up of genuine characters who were personable, entertaining, forceful, and each in his or her own way quite talented. The men were good with animals and looked larger than life on horseback. The women were capable at cooking, canning, putting up, and setting by, and did not stand for much foolishness.

It seems likely a young man trying to get started in life, like I imagine my father was, could get overshadowed by these people. At any rate, my father went his own way, and I was left with a story of throwing up on him once and my mother's explanation of her fear he would not be able to take care of us.

When my mother finally did strike out on her own, I began my dual life in white and Indian worlds. The two places were vastly different in many ways. Fort Belknap had a rich history; Shelby was an oil boomtown.

My mother took me with her, but with the encouragement of my grandmother and aunt, and out of my love for the ranch, I returned there, living with my mother only when I had to attend school. By the age of twelve I was adept at getting myself back and forth by bus, train, mail truck, relatives, and acquaintances.

Traveling back and forth made me independent at a young age, and I still don't like to stay in one place all the time. It also created distance between me and my mother, and between me and other people. I never felt abandoned, or like I was being farmed out; I just developed a taste for being gone at times, and the women of my childhood indulged me in this.

The women of my family are Gros Ventres, Falls people, Atsina, White Clay people, The People of Many Names, of the Otter Robe family, Black Lodge Clan. My great-grandmother Otter Robe would have been among the first generation of Gros Ventres to live on the high plains after they were driven from Lake Winnipeg by the Crees, who had obtained guns through fur trade with the French.

My great-grandfather Louis Chambeaux was a New Orleans Cajun whose family migrated up the Mississippi to St. Paul when he was a child. For his twelfth birthday his father gave him a pony, whereupon he promptly ran away to Dakota territory, where he lived with the Turtle Mountain people in the Dakotas until early adulthood. After working as a cowboy throughout the western United States, he settled at Beaver Creek, near present-day Havre, Montana, where he worked as a scout and packer for the U.S. Army at Fort Assinniboine.

Meadowhawk, Blackbird, Thorn, Bull Calf

When Chief Joseph of the Nez Perce disappeared after routing U.S. troops at the Battle of the Big Hole, General Miles sent for him (his name had been changed by the army paymaster to Shambo by then), and he found Joseph at Snake Creek in the Bearpaw Mountains, where the Battle of the Bear's Paw took place. A. J. Noyes, in his book *The Life of Shambow,* related that the old man said, "I never did like that SOB Miles, but I did it in the line of duty."

In later years my great-grandmother returned to her people at Fort Belknap. My grandmother Maggie, who was raised by housekeepers and in government schools, also eventually returned to Fort Belknap. She married Seth Burtch, a white man from Kansas, who was foreman of the Stevens ranch. They settled on her allotted land just east of People's Creek and had six children of their own and made a living raising horses, cattle, and hay. Their ranch is still located on the northeastern corner of the Fort Belknap Reservation, within a small area naturally flood-irrigated by runoff from the Little Rocky Mountains.

This natural irrigation system enabled my family and two others, the Stevenses and the Ereauxs, to be relatively prosperous for that area. All three families were comprised of Indian women and white men who settled on the women's allotted land. These people were unique enough at Fort Belknap that they gained their own identities as "the Dodson Indians" (named after the nearby town of Dodson, Montana) as distinguished from the Mountain Indians to the south and the Agency/River Indians to the west.

Indian on one side, white on the other, my family were generally known as "breeds" but were nonetheless typical reservation people. My grandmother spoke Gros Ventre, my aunt served on the tribal council, and we raised cattle and hay for a living. We were not as traditional as some but kept in touch with Indian ways through the council, the Sun Dance and other ceremonies, and our ties to relatives and friends on the reservation. We worked very hard and identified strongly with what we perceived to be a "modern Indian" way of life.

In contrast to Fort Belknap was Shelby. Approximately one hundred and seventy miles west of Fort Belknap, Shelby was the site of the Dempsey-Gibbons fight in the twenties, where the entire town went broke promoting a world championship heavyweight boxing match. The town was made up mainly of farmers and other working people, about fifty-five hundred in population in its heyday.

Shelby had eleven bars—the Oil City, Oasis, Elks, Turks, Alibi, Teegarden's, Sports Club, Tap Room, Vets, Eagles, and the Dixie Inn. The town was hard-drinking, sports crazy, and probably dysfunctional in some ways by today's standards. There was very little sympathy for minorities, which meant Indians, in that area; it was a place where "Dogs and Indians Not Allowed" signs were posted in earnest until nearly mid-century.

At Fort Belknap I learned about ranching, Indian ways, the land, and family values. I lived there for nearly thirty years and still go back on a regular basis. In Shelby I learned about the American educational system, race and class, and competing for a place in the great baby-boom generation. I graduated from high school there but haven't been back much since.

From both, however, I learned what it meant to belong to two different worlds at the same time and to live with a degree of non-acceptance by both. One of my earliest memories is of being turned away from the Bureau of Indian Affairs hospital at the agency because I was not enrolled as a member of the Gros Ventre tribe. It was not chic to be Indian at the time, and my family thought it best not to make waves about enrollment until I turned up seriously ill one winter.

Although an adoptive aunt, Aggie Adams, eventually got my medical dilemma changed by force of will, confusion characterized my relationship with the Bureau of Indian Affairs, which was an important connection in terms of goods and services. Although I received medical treatment and a few commodities, I have never been able to convince anyone in authority to help with what eventually became the most sustained activity of my life—education. I am Indian and I am not, as near as I can figure.

I changed schools at the beginning of fourth grade. During that first recess a boy approached me, and I struck out at him just in case he was thinking of doing it to me. Nine years is young to be so cynical, but I had learned to strike first or clear out when in doubt. Moving back and forth between places and cultures was partly the reason for that kind of reaction. Oftentimes I was an outsider and found myself fighting for acceptance.

I was also insecure about my life away from the ranch. My family at Fort Belknap was very strongly centered in the land and in the community, and I knew who I was there. In Shelby we were newcomers, outsiders, people of little status, and I was always afraid someone would find out. The sense of fragmentation made me edgy, and at times I lashed out from the weight of it.

Fortunately, I had some athletic ability, and athletics eventually became a focus for that part of my life. I had a coach in high school who took an interest in me, a man named Terry Radcliffe, who also taught senior English. He had a lot of technical knowledge about sports and also took the time to pass on larger concepts only loosely related to competition. He had a kind of Zen-like approach to running and was always preaching to us about the value of getting the elements of running straight in our minds before we actually went onto the track. Training under Radcliffe included such things as morning workouts, intended not so much for conditioning as to get the day started properly, as well as his regimen of vitamins.

I overheard him praising me to another coach once, and that was very different than being called a smart aleck or short-tempered. He named me captain of the track team, and I worked very hard to live up to that responsibility. He made the study of English interesting and that was a godsend. I saw him as intellectual as well as physical, and the balance was captivating. I responded with long-term involvements in sports and education.

Later, a number of Indian writers helped me with a long-standing feeling of being faced with the task of dealing with a world too complicated for anybody my size. These writers helped by portraying worlds in which personal choice and action count. More and more Indian writers have taken on this role by documenting the special place of minority perception in American society—allowing the reader to become part of Indian experiences with their full shares of social despair and individual energy.

I write from a position of illegitimacy, an exquisite place from which to consider legitimacy. I have no father, I am part Indian, I am not wealthy, and I choose to live a life of the mind, all "illegitimacies" in one setting or another. Gros Ventres reduce illegitimacy to a phrase. They call illegitimate children "Catch Colt," the term for an unplanned horse pregnancy, and within certain bounds they often go to some effort to help "Catch Colts" have a fair chance in life.

Viewed in a more positive light, I feel that my background is incredibly rich and represents what I understand to be authentic experience, and that is important. Having already been humbled by circumstance, I do not seek to privilege any particular point of view or to pit any person against anyone else. Instead, I like to try to use a unique set of experiences to show that everyone can talk to everyone else.

My favorite aunt—they called her Sister—was a pretty girl with dark hair and a wide, even smile. She told me once of standing in the kitchen door watching my grandmother flirt with Smith O'Bryan when he came to the ranch one day to sharpen his mower sickles.

Sis said my grandmother told her repeatedly to go check some plums boiling on the stove for jelly. She said she knew what they were doing and wouldn't leave them alone, and that was like her. She was very strong-minded, and in that regard she resembled my grandmother.

My grandmother left Seth Burtch in the thirties, citing his orneriness and spitting on the floor among her reasons. I suspect the fact she was in love with Smith O'Bryan also had something to do with it, but love didn't count for much in that country. Acting right did, and my grandmother's defection must have been as controversial as hell. I still remember her complaints, including the allegation that being married to Seth was like being married to *The Saturday Evening Post.*

One of my earliest memories is of my grandmother insisting to my aunt that I could read the Golden Book version of *Bambi* when I was maybe four years old. My aunt was skeptical and insisted that I show her. I performed passably as I recall but it could have been because I knew the story by heart. Reading was serious business. My grandmother resented my grandfather's reading. The Bureau of Indian Affairs read to the Indian people what would happen to them. My aunt insisted reading was crucial to being able to get along in the modern world.

I often wondered how my grandmother felt about Smith O'Bryan's appetite for paperback westerns compared to Seth Burtch's reading habit. She seemed to think reading was self-indulgent as well as valuable, and that created some confusion about where the line should be drawn in favor of getting work done.

I knew Seth Burtch through my Aunt Sis's reverence for him and other stories that made him sound like John Wesley Hardin, who, according to *Wild West* magazine, once shot a man to death for snoring. Smith O'Bryan was the grandfather I knew personally. He was big and red, a quiet man who automatically extended his arm to hoist me up next to him when I came near. He laughed when I sat on his lap steering his '57 Ranchero all over the highway on the way to town. Later, I took him for a drive most Sundays while I was in high school, lifting him up off the floor when he began to fall out of his chair in restaurants where we stopped for pie. I read many of his books along with him when I was young, bewitching myself with the nineteenth-century myth they reflected of the romantic loner on the boundless frontier. It was calm and orderly at my grandmother's place by the time I came along. She kept her yard fenced with barbed wire and mowed the spear grass with a little yellow push mower. The haying equipment was lined up in a neat row next to a wooden granary between the house and the barn where Smith kept his horses. When he could still get around he rode out early in the morning to check his cattle, returning by lunchtime. In the afternoon he ate and read while my grandmother puttered around keeping herself busy. In the evening they walked through the turnstile in the fence and sat in the outhouse together. It was different at my aunt's. The clutter of years was piled everywhere. Machinery sat wherever it had been shut off the year before. My uncle's tools were scattered around inside his pickup, some under the seat, and others buried under musty hay in the box. At the same time there existed a curious kind of order. Both my aunt and uncle knew exactly where everything was, and especially if something was missing. I think the mess was a smokescreen in a way. It was hard to have things when so many others had nothing.

It was even more different at my mother's home. She was raised by five older brothers and sisters after my grandmother left, and she grew up spoiled and kind of deprived all at once. It seems clear the older children had prior claims on such things as the ranch, but my mother had her own resource in her beauty, which was considerable, and that played a large part in enabling her to make a life of her own. Although she was not educated beyond junior high school, she was intelligent in a way my Aunt Sis once described as "cunning," a considerable compliment from her shrewd older sister.

Catch Colt

My family liked kids, which allowed younger folks to move freely among grandparents, aunts and uncles, family friends, and brothers and sisters of all kinds. Five of us took up more or less permanent residence at my aunt's place. Three were the sons of Burtch sisters, one was my uncle's nephew, and one was my cousin-brother Neil's daughter. In addition, I had a half-brother, a stepsister, and a bunch of other cousins who lived elsewhere.

I was the youngest boy by nearly fifteen years, and the older boys by turns tortured me and taught me things they knew. My uncle hauled household water in a large galvanized barrel that sat on a stoneboat in front of the kitchen door. I can't recall how many times I got dunked headfirst in that barrel by one of the older boys holding me by my ankles, but it was plenty. They also taught me how to work stock, to hunt, to drive, and, most importantly, to laugh.

At my mother's place I was the oldest and passed on good and ill as I had learned them. In other settings I was a guest, a cousin, a nephew. These combinations, oppositions, and inversions were part of a complex family structure that extended itself into my life like tentacles.

Leslie Silko has said, "You should understand the way it was back then, because it is the same even now." Back then begins for me when I was about five years old. I can remember kneeling on a saddle in the middle of my grandmother's kitchen floor, roping a red Hills Brothers coffee can with a piece of baling twine. My grandmother busied herself in the kitchen, talking to me all the while. In the other room my grandfather sat cross-legged, his shirt collar buttoned at the neck, reading a paperback western.

Meadowhawk, Blackbird, Thorn, Bull Calf

It might have appeared that my grandmother was talking absentmindedly and that I was not paying much attention. But she had chosen her words with the unconscious wisdom of age and experience, and I remember many things she said with a clarity associated with the first stories I ever heard.

"My father, your great-grandfather, worked for the government at Fort Assinniboine for many years," my grandmother said once, marching from stove to sink. "He was a packer and scout. It was the government that changed our name to S-h-a-m-b-o. They spelled it wrong in the payroll office. He decided to leave it that way so that if he got into trouble his folks wouldn't suffer for it.

"When those Nez Perce left Idaho they raised cain with the soldiers. General Miles finally got desperate and sent for my father to help him. His orders were to find Joseph and his people. He found them just past Snake Creek in the Bearpaws.

"He said he wasn't proud of it, but it was in the line of duty. He said those Nez Perce were the best fighters he ever saw, and he had lived with Indian people since he ran away from Saint Paul when he was twelve. That would have been in about '48.

"I tell you this because I want you to know your people amount to something. And I don't want you to be like these Indians around here. I want you to get out of here and go to school."

Sensing a seam in the storytelling, I seized the opportunity to interject. Although I was very young, I already knew how to tease my grandmother just enough to make her laugh. "Gramma, if you loan me your .22, I'll shoot those magpies that are stealing your eggs," I said.

"Oh you!" she chuckled, stopping to look at me carefully.

"There's plenty of time for you to learn how to shoot. And don't you dare touch that gun by yourself. You can have your own when you're twelve. It took all of us to raise you so far, and I don't want you shooting yourself now. Besides, your mother and her man are coming to take you to the fair tomorrow."

"Those magpies are getting fat," I replied. My grandmother stopped and looked at me again, surprised at the grown-up sounding words. "You just go on and don't bother me anymore. I'm trying to cook here," she said. She had lured me in earlier for tea and homemade bread with real butter.

My mother and Leon came the next day to pick me up. They were all dressed up, him in a white shirt and new Levi's, her in a turquoise western shirt and black saddle pants. She had long black hair, dark eyes, and perfect big white teeth.

My brother Gary and stepsister Judy were with my mother and Leon, and the three of us sat in the back seat of the car playing grab-ass as we pulled away from the house. Leon's good nature disappeared as soon as the house was out of sight, and he yelled at us to knock it off.

We had fun on the midway in the afternoon. Silver dollars weighted us down, and we protected our money carefully from the barkers as we walked among the skin games and whirling rides. There were couples with teddy bears walking entwined with each other; other couples with real children looked harried and tired; a kid with a huge head sat half in and half out of a wheelchair smiling happily at the passing crowd.

Evening came, a luxurious blue darkening to black that set off the bright neon lights of the carnival. The fair seemed to catch its breath and plunge ahead again, refreshed, into the remote Montana night.

It was about nine o'clock when Leon drove us from the fairgrounds past the bars that faced Highway 2. He parked the '54 Plymouth in front of Wally's, and my mother made a bed in the back seat. She went inside and brought out pop and potato chips and told us not to leave the car. Bobby Gray and Babe Ereaux stopped on their way into Wally's and gave us quarters; then they all went back into the bar. As the door swung open we could see people laughing and drinking in the colored light. "Too many times married men think they're still single" wafted out from the jukebox, then was cut off by the closing door.

Bobby Gray was small and good-looking. He always wore white shirts with the cuffs folded back on his forearms and held his beer nearly to his armpit with the hand turned inward. I asked him once why he did that. He said he held his hands that way to train himself to keep his knuckles out so he could hit harder. He had unusual self-confidence and physical ability that was astounding for his size. People either liked him or disliked him very much—there seemed to be no in-between.

It was later on when Bobby Gray and a big white cowboy exploded out the front door of Wally's onto the sidewalk, lit in soft blues and reds from the neon beer signs in the blinded windows. The cowboy slammed his hat down on the concrete, talking mean and swinging crazily; he looked like he intended to kill Bobby. Bobby didn't seem to do much in response to the cowboy's wild actions. He only looked annoyed at the flailing charges that caused him to step back or sideways, then resumed his position directly in front of the cowboy. He seemed to hypnotize the cow-

boy with sharp, side-to-side movements of his head, his fists lick-
ing out only occasionally as if to measure the distance of ribs and
jaw.

Then a strange thing happened. The cowboy doubled his
charges, and as he was clubbing Bobby with huge hairy arms, it
was his nose instead that suddenly blossomed scarlet; as he
punched and swore it was his shirt that turned dark red in the
neon light, and he began to shrink. It was a slight sagging at first,
then he collapsed to one knee, then to his hands and knees, then
flat on his back where his loud breath rasped and gurgled gobbets
of blood out of his shattered mouth. Bobby Gray, larger than the
cowboy now, grinned and walked through the crowd back into
the bar. His shirt was still white.

I slid down from the roof of the car, through the open window,
and into the back seat. I lay on a pillow opposite Gary and Judy
and curled a bottle of 7-Up into my armpit. My hand curved inward with the small knuckles sticking out. Further down U.S.
Highway 2 to the east another bar sign flashed over and over
again, Big 2, Big 2, Big 2.

I have a picture of Gary, Judy, and me from that time, taken at
my grandmother's house before we left for the fair. We are all
dressed up and smiling the happy dumb smiles of small children.
Ten months after those pictures were taken, Leon was killed in the
same car we drove to the fair that summer. A few months after
that, Judy ended up in a Montana orphanage called Mooseheart.

I have known fear in my life—deep, paralyzing fear that stayed
with me for weeks. This kind of fear is not the spontaneous alarm
associated with surprise that comes and goes quickly. It is something that has to be learned over a period of time under the right

circumstances. I learned lasting fear during the time my mother made the transition from Fort Belknap to Shelby.

Although Leon was part of the transition, I don't really know much about him. He was a Turtle Mountain Chippewa, short and stocky, and wore his hair slicked back. He tended bar at the Moose Club and had some relatives in Shelby we used to visit. He and my mother argued about his being at the bar when he wasn't working. I took my mother's side one time in that snotty way kids have, and I remember running from him then, knowing that if he caught me he would hurt me. I was five years old.

Then he was dead, and there was a small jar of change on the kitchen windowsill that the undertaker had removed from his pockets. I remember my mother's fear when he was dead. I knew even then it wasn't grief but fear of what would happen to her and three small children, and that scared me, too.

I remember being afraid for my stepsister Judy when she went to stay with Art Doolittle. Art Doolittle was a janitor at the Meadowlark grade school, and he and his wife wanted a child. Somehow they got Judy, but before that winter was over she was in an orphanage. I was afraid that if that could happen to her, maybe it could happen to me, too.

In the spring I had a tonsillectomy. A couple of days later, during the recovery period, a nurse gave me a big shot of penicillin, contrary to the instructions on my chart, and blood started to spurt from my nose. As I was being rushed back to the operating room I remember Ralph W. Jennings, M.D., bleating, "Jesus Christ, he's bleeding to death, what are we going to do?" That scared me so bad I passed out. I was six years old.

I am not sure I want to know much more about those years

than I do. I saw some things go seriously wrong. I saw a community that did not know how to take care of its weak and un-protected, that only knew to keep demanding they pay their bills. I saw men trail my mother like hounds, thinking they finally had her where they wanted her.

Although the life we led together was at times not what I wanted for either one of us, I have nothing but respect for my mother. We might not appear to be very close, but we share a strong bond of family and experience. I don't ask her what happened to Judy. I don't care why she gave her beauty to men who seemed so undeserving. We survived those vulnerable years in a town that was struggling as much as we were to deal with cultural difference, and that is enough.

We not only survived but began to pick up speed. My mother got a job, I regained my health; nobody died, disappeared, or went nuts on us for awhile. Fear was replaced by peevishness at not being better off than we were.

But that wasn't the way it was at the ranch. There we had horses and cars, and nobody messed with the clannish bunch comprised of Burtches mixed with Coles, Bears, and God knows who else, because it was just plain dangerous. One of my cousin-brothers, Skip, made violence an art form when he got his size. He was tough, smart, and had a Burtch trait of being able to become slightly unhinged.

More than once I have heard that sound that is like no other, the sound of bone on bone, and looked around to see someone laying in a heap at Skip's feet. He got in a fight in Wally's at Dodson Fair one time and Delwin Simms, who was bouncing that night, got him in a full nelson from the back. Just as it looked as if

Skip's neck would snap with the force of being bent forward, he knocked Simms out with one punch thrown blind and backwards behind his head.

Skip's excitability was not always as entertaining as watching him fight. Working with him was like I imagine working with explosives would be. You had to pay attention or you were liable to get demolished. He took off after a ringy old cow in his pickup one time when we were working cattle. The country was rough, and when he returned, about half an hour later, the pickup's stock rack and hood were missing, the radiator was leaking, and one side was all bashed in. The cow, of course, was dead.

At the same time, Skip was a very loving, caring, giving person. He taught me how to drive and how to heel calves on horseback. When I left the ranch, he came to visit me in the places I lived. He died of kidney failure, probably brought on by a bout with strep throat when he was in the army, the doctors said. As my Aunt Sis and I were taking a last look at him at the funeral home she said, "It's too bad we had to lose our boy." And it was.

Life at Fort Belknap, although very physical and sometimes violent, seemed heroic compared to what seemed to be a kind of hopelessness I observed in other places I lived. The Indians may have been the remnants of a defeated culture, but they still had more going for them than the wage slaves plugged into the banking system off-reservation. My family reflected a kind of heroism, and I loved them for it.

Otter Robe Women

Woods Aakre built my grandmother's new house. She had a new house, an old house, a chicken house, a springhouse, and an outhouse. Houses were important to her. Aakre had done well, beginning with the granite mining boom at Snake Butte south of Harlem. He supplied ties for the rail spur out there and materials to build houses and bars for the laborers who moved in to work for the government. Success made him creative. One of the things he did was promote two-room frame houses, built on-site, to Indians and other dryland farmers for a couple thousand dollars apiece.

My grandmother secured one of these houses shortly after she left Seth Burtch and their six wild-ass children and married Smith O'Bryan. She kept the house fenced in and fresh painted white with green trim, with newspapers in the south windows to keep the sun out. It had no plumbing or insulation, but it was a good place to entertain notions of civilization. Smith liked to read in there, behind the newspapers where it was cool. He was not much for anything but horses, cattle, and reading. He left everything else to my grandmother.

It might have been because Seth was so ornery, or that Smith was a ladies' man, but my grandmother loved Smith and liked to do for him, although she didn't like people to know it. "Get up now, and bring me some water," she said to him one day.

He groaned and got up out of his reclining chair to look for his romeo slippers. They had elastic in the sides and looked like elf shoes. Outside, the cottonwood leaves rattled in a slight breeze. Magpies dived and braked around the barn, squawking loudly. There was the metallic sound of a pail handle as the screen door slammed.

"There's a hole in the bucket," he said, returning empty-handed.

"Well, fix it," my grandmother said, marching toward her treadle sewing machine.

"What should I fix it with?" he asked, examining the rusted-through spot carefully.

"Make a plug from that piece of wood in the porch by my hammer," she said.

The magpies were closer now, perched on the little John Deere tractor parked between the house and the barn. One of them was fighting to retain his hold on the steering wheel while two others attacked him in shifts.

"This here is too long," Smith said, turning a piece of cedar between his large fingers.

"Well, cut it," replied my grandmother.

"Cut it with what?" he said.

"There's an axe in the corner behind your chaps," she said.

She had moved to the kitchen window and was eying the magpies and her chicken coop, which stood off to the side by the riverbank.

"This axe is pretty dull," Smith said, sitting down at the kitchen table.

"Well, sharpen it," she said, opening the oven door of her Monarch electric stove.

"With what?" he said.

"The grindstone is out in the granary," she said.

A magpie swooped through the yard and lit on a fence post in front of the back door. My grandmother dropped a pan she had begun greasing and wheeled for the porch, wiping her hands on her apron furiously.

She returned with a battered single-shot .22 rifle and a couple of brass and gray bullets clenched in her teeth. She broke the rifle open and inserted a bullet as she tiptoed to the back door. Locking the breech again, she raised the rifle to the magpie teetering in the breeze on top of the fence post, his head swiveling crazily as he eyed the house and the chicken coop simultaneously. The rifle cracked as she shot through the screen, and the magpie fell to the ground in a heap.

"What the hell's going on?" Smith asked, walking back in the front door.

"Oh," he said to himself as he looked through the screen door at the scene beyond, then walked back out.

Outside, my grandmother, wearing Smith's bright yellow Handy Andy gloves, was transporting the dead magpie to the dump over the riverbank. She had it in a scoop shovel and looked like some kind of colorful bird herself as she perched at the bank looking at the refuse below.

"That grindstone's awful dry," Smith said as he joined my grandmother at the riverbank to watch the breeze ruffle the shiny feathers jutting at odd angles. As they walked back to the house, past the outhouse and through the turnstile in the fence, the Milk River shouldered its way around the big bend and on to Hartman's place below. The remaining two magpies, together now, squawked in unison from safety.

"Well, put some water on it then," my grandmother said as she peered the distance up to Smith's big red face. "There's a hole in the bucket," he replied deadpan, turning his head away from her and grinning into the distance toward his cattle, grazing off in the light yellow hills somewhere. Years later I heard his joke again in an old folk song on a Harry Belafonte record and it reminded me of how much I didn't think he knew.

"Gramma, get my clothes, will you?" I said. "I'm going to go stay with Nee-Stoh for awhile."

"Nee-Stoh, huh?" My grandmother smiled at my use of her oldest daughter's Indian name. As she looked over her glasses at me she seemed to measure how I had begun to grow angular and skinny.

"Yes, I want to talk to Neil."

"Important business, is it?" She smiled again, fooling with a pattern she was pinning to some cloth.

"Why don't you stay here and trap that weasel like you said you would."

"Gramma, Neil told me that weasel was good to have around," I replied.

"So, Neil said that, did he?" Neil and I shared favored grandchild status with her.

"That's the way of it, though," she said, her face inches from the sewing machine needle as her left hand worked the wheel. "Nobody wants to stay with old people."

"I do," I said, falling into a familiar trap.

"No you don't," she said. "You'll go off like all the rest, and I'll be left with no one to take care of me when I can't do for myself."

"I'll take care of you Gramma," I said, putting my long arm around her shoulders, "if you'll get my clothes and put them in a sack." I had played this game before.

"My stars," she laughed. "You're nothing but a pest."

"I know," I said, "and I need to eat before I go."

"Good grief," she muttered, flailing the air with a folded paper grocery bag as she tried to get it open.

"Why don't you ride Steel over there," she said. "I don't like that black thing Smith insists on letting you ride."

"Think I could borrow his saddlebags?" I countered.

"Don't change the subject. That horse likes to shy."

"It would be a lot easier to carry my stuff," I said.

"If you lose those saddlebags Smith will skin you alive."

"You can pick them up Friday when you go to town," I said, knowing the old man wouldn't.

Steel was old and gray, a horse my mother had told me she rode when she was a girl. He was reliable but slow, and mainly did what he wanted. I liked the black; it was small and fast, and loved to run.

It was true I didn't have much in common with the old gray horse, except for my mother. I looked out for him because of that and made sure he got oats when the others did. My mother and I lived in different worlds much of the time, and I often wondered what she was doing. It was a habit I had developed, wondering about my mother, and my father, whom I had never seen. I sometimes imagined my father turning off the highway one day, turning off and stopping to see me.

"I'm going to saddle up; then I'll come back and eat," I said, trying to hurry my grandmother along.

"If you must," she sighed. "Water the chickens while you're out there, will you?"

"Okay," I said.

There were five horses in the small field next to the barn. I opened the gate to the round corral and walked out to one side. It was hot and a slight breeze rustled the cottonwood leaves, stirring up smells of sagebrush, manure, and stagnant slough water.

As soon as I got behind the horses they took off for the barn. I ran behind them and closed the gate, which was big and had sagged over the years so that I had to drag it through the dirt. I dug my heels into the deep layer of sun-baked manure that covered the natural soil and pulled the gate shut by jerks. I tied the gate shut with baling wire and noticed that my cowboy boots were about shot. Summer was almost over.

The round corral was nearly eight feet high, constructed of large poles laid on top of each other and supported by railroad ties. It was actually more of a hexagon, built that way so there were no sharp corners, and sturdy enough to hold a fifteen-hundred-pound animal going full speed. There was a two-foot thick snubbing post in the center, worn shiny by the action of rope on its surface.

As I went into the barn the horses bunched on the opposite side of the corral, snorting and milling around. It was cool and dark inside, and smelled like leather and hay. Saddles hung from a ceiling joist on one end, with an assortment of ropes, bridles, and other equipment hanging from nails driven into the wall studs. I looked around carefully for rattlesnakes as I moved inside.

I took a rope down from the wall and shook out a loop. It was stiff and gray, the nylon twist fuzzy from use. There was a kink in it, so I tossed it on the floor and twirled it around in circles until it straightened out.

The bright square of light at the door darkened as one of the horses stuck his head inside. I coiled the rope back into my left hand and built another loop as I walked back outside, sliding the big door shut behind me. The old gray horse moved his muzzle close, looking for grain. He knew he was not the one I was after.

Any of these would come to a coffee can with grain in it, but that was no fun; I liked to rope them the way Smith did in the spring, when they were snuffy from their winter's rest.

I walked to the center of the corral and the horses began to move to my left. Even old Steel caught the spirit, and soon they

29

were charging wildly around the enclosure. I moved into them until they made a single, circling line, then I began to turn with the black. I got the horse's rhythm, swung the loop hard to give it life, then snaked it around the sleek neck.

As soon as he felt the pressure, the black stopped in his tracks and walked obediently toward me. We had been through this many times before, and the choreography was nearly perfect. I rushed to get the battered old Association saddle, the kind approved for saddle bronc riding at rodeos, on. The smells and sights of the barnyard were satisfying. In the hot afternoon I felt like a good cowboy and part of all that surrounded me.

I pulled the latigo tight, then hurried out of the corral to the pump. I hung on the long rusty-brown handle to get the water flowing, then jumped and hung again and again to fill the five-gallon Conoco grease bucket. I wondered how my grandmother did it as I wrestled the water to the chicken coop and splashed it into the tires the chickens drank from. I also wondered how anyone could cut a tire in half like that.

I went back into the house and pulled a chair back from the table. There were small quantities of food set out. The old people ate that way—little things all day long.

"Take off your hat and wash your hands," my grandmother said.

"Gramma, you know what?" I said as I poured water in the white enamel wash basin. It had a red rim, a couple of black chips, and a small nut and bolt through its side where a leak had been fixed.

"No, what?"

"Me and Neil are going hunting for prairie chickens."

"You just make sure he doesn't take you to Zortman hunting for those Bear girls."

"No, Gramma. Neil said he saw a whole bunch of them over on the Strikes At forty," I said, my mouth stuffed full of food.

"Well, bring me some then, but clean them first," she said. "And have some tea to wash that down before you choke."

I sat and chewed then, happy to think about going hunting. My grandmother talked at me steadily as I ate, but I was lost in my own thoughts. I finished and grabbed a pair of embossed saddlebags hanging over a chair back.

"Gramma, I have to go before it gets dark," I said.

"You be careful going across that ditch now, do you hear? It's a good thing Steel knows the way."

"Ya, Gram," I said, sliding out the door sideways.

I walked quickly toward the barn, turned and went backward for awhile, then ran the last few yards with the heavy bags tangling around my ankles. I tied the bags to the rear saddle strings, then led the black horse through the gate. I walked him around in a circle a couple of times the way Smith did with his broncs, then swung into the saddle and rode back toward the house.

The black horse pranced sideways, neck bowed. My grandmother was inside her barbed-wire fence, bent over a pile of newspapers she was tying up with string. I pulled up even with her, then yelled and relaxed my grip on the reins.

My grandmother turned around, surprised, then put her hands on her hips and scowled as she realized which horse I was riding. She raised her finger and shook it a couple of times, then raised her hand to her forehead to shade her eyes and watch us tear out across the hayfield. We slowed at the irrigation ditch, stopped, turned, and I waved at her. She waved back and went into the house.

As the screen door closed I wheeled the horse and started him toward a weathered wooden bridge that spanned the ditch. He was short-coupled, with the muscular rump of a quarter horse. He had a way of walking like he was on ice when he didn't want to do something, and as he began to gyrate I brought the ends of the reins down across his flank.

In the short space of a moment the horse gathered himself, made a huge leap forward, then sucked back to a place behind where he had started. I was left stretched out in midair at the exact point where the horse had changed direction. I hung there for a second or two, then dropped to the ground.

I popped up immediately, like a gopher out of a hole, and looked back toward the house. Alfalfa windrows bristled in my vision where the rough stalks had been turned up to the sky; the smell was heavy and warm. I couldn't see my grandmother, so I hurriedly pulled a piece of oil cake out of my pocket and extended it in the palm of my hand.

My grandmother was an Otter Robe woman, granddaughter of Otter Robe of the Black Lodge, a war clan of the White Clay people. She had power, power to raise the musty alfalfa, power to stay dignified in a foolish world, power to make a child proud so that he couldn't stand for her to see him get bucked off.

I approached the black horse slowly, talking in a soothing voice. The horse's front legs were spread wide; his breath roared through his red nostrils. His ears worked back and forth as he observed carefully to see what was going to happen.

"You little sonofabitch," I crooned. The words I had learned

32

from my older cousin-brothers were big for my skinny body. I tried to think what Wink would do. He was the best horseman of us all, and ranchers from all around used to bring spoiled horses for him to ride.

Wink was my other cousin-brother. He was my Uncle Buck's nephew and had been adopted by Buck and my Aunt Sis, unlike Skip and I, who had more or less adopted them. Good-natured and even-tempered, he was also the one neighbors came to get when they wanted a horse colt castrated properly. "I'm gonna tie you up and give you post hay and injun' lovin' until your head falls through your asshole."

The horse nickered at the gentle sounding words and took a tentative step forward as two blackbirds skittered up the ditch and flared over some cattails. Ignoring them, he made a couple of false starts, then stretched his neck out to lip the smooth pellet of ground barley into his mouth. At the same time, I gathered the reins in a smooth motion with my other hand.

Looking over my shoulder again, I led the black horse to the bridge and walked him across. The horse paid no attention this time, chewing the oil cake noisily as we clattered over the worn planks. I sometimes ate the stuff myself, enjoying the sweet taste of the molasses that held it together. It was good as long as you didn't bite into a place a mouse had pissed on.

Out of sight on the other side of the ditch, the horse and I walked awhile. I thought about the propriety of getting back on, and there was a moment when I wanted badly to go back to the little white house with its green trim, to turn the black horse loose and help my grandmother with her sewing. Then the feeling was gone, and I stopped, turned the oxbow stirrup backward, and swung up. The black horse shook his head, sneezed, then moved out smoothly. I felt immediate and overwhelming relief.

The patchwork quilt of hayfields on the way to Nee-Stoh's was like a series of well-kept little parks separated by winding strands of red willow that followed the irrigation ditches. The fields were connected by obscure pickup trails through the heavy growth. In these narrow spots the willows were stripped bone-white from being run over. In the fall, when the haying was done, the undercarriage of Smith's pickup would be worn shiny from driving around in there.

It was lush and tropical along the river bottom, but in the brown hills only a mile or two away, sparrows huddled in the narrow shade thrown by fence posts, their sharp tongues sticking out of mouths wide open against the heat. As the afternoon light dimmed almost imperceptibly, I nudged the horse into a trot, for I was reminded that mosquitoes would start swarming as soon as the air cooled. I stood in the stirrups, the saddle horn cupped under both hands, and leaned forward, absorbing the rough gait in my arms and legs.

No cattle were in the valley in the summer, and the gates were open for the haying crews. I was glad, knowing that a closed gate would give the black horse another chance to stand me on my head.

My aunt had told me once that the reason there were so many mosquitoes in the summer was to drive the animals out to the hills, so they could come back to the valley where there was shelter in the winter as well as food. It made sense to me as I glimpsed the steeply pitched roof of her house in the distance.

At People's Creek I reined into the smooth ruts of a road worn into the black, spongy gumbo. It was like cake and yielded to the weight of the horse. When it rained, the stuff absorbed so much water it became like heavy grease and was impassable. The road led to a rocky crossing in the creek, and we splashed out into the middle and stopped.

The horse stretched his neck impatiently against the reins a couple of times, then lowered his head and drank a deep, sucking belly full of water. He raised his tail and farted. The sound scared him and he splayed his legs out stiffly on the wet rocks, blowing through his nostrils as water ran out of his mouth. "Oh shit," I thought, and urged him on warily. He slipped and slid across to the other side.

An orange Eddy's Bread truck was laboring across the flat as we came up out of the creek. Its tires sang against the hot asphalt that looked like shimmering water in the distance. Its mud flaps danced like skirts as it crossed in front of the house and began to climb the hill to the east.

The truck shifted gears as it climbed, slowing nearly to a halt before it inched over the top and disappeared down the other side. It passed through here twice a day during the week. I always listened carefully, thinking someday it wouldn't make the hill. I also thought that this highway would bring my father someday, and I could not imagine that event never coming to pass.

The black horse scrabbled up the approach to the highway, his hooves grinding and squeaking in the gravel. I grabbed the horn as he rolled his eyes at the striped surface, then lunged across. On the other side he stretched out into a lope toward the house, whinnying loudly.

Through the wind in my eyes I could see the heads of horses

stretched over corral poles, their ears cocked sharply forward. At the wooden gate I jumped down, loosening the cinch behind the stirrup leather on the go. I pulled the saddle down, then reached up and pulled the bridle off as the horse bumped through the crooked opening. Once through, he trotted proudly to the others, tail held high in the air, and bumped noses with a hammer-headed bay called Mickey.

I bent down and hoisted my tack onto my shoulder, the saddle blanket wet and pungent on my arm. I walked toward the house, a stirrup knocking hard against the bone of my knee. I loved leaving and arriving, the overlap of a cycle of movement that gave me room to breathe, not to have to stay in one place too long.

The saddle was heavy, and I struggled to the bunkhouse, threw open the screen door, and looked around. It was a man's place, with beds, ashtrays, and adventure magazines. On one end, among a jumble of saddles, guns, cowboy boots with socks sticking out, and some horseshoeing equipment, stood a wood stove. A bad oil painting of a cowboy roping a coyote hung slightly crooked on the painted Sheetrock wall. I added my things to the variety of objects and walked back out into the sunshine.

I could hear my Aunt Sis banging pots around in the kitchen of the big house as I stepped inside.

"Oh, it's you!" she said, smiling broadly as she wiped back a wisp of hair from her damp forehead.

"Come in and have some ice tea!" I loved the quick happiness on her face, and her obvious affection for me.

The kitchen had belonged to my grandmother once, as had this whole house. It had been her original homestead shack, but now it was tacked on to the front of the log house she had built by

selling some of the fine sorrel horses her father had left her when
he died.

I walked smiling into the cool interior of the house. Having
lived through the depression when there was no money, and when
things were often not available even if there was money, my aunt
saved everything. There were Congressional Records from when
she was on the Tribal Council, Stetson hat boxes with no Stetsons
in them, clothes hanging from doorframes, Christmas cards
propped up in corners, piles of letters tied up in piles, and canned
goods on the floor in boxes.

I flopped down on a couch covered with a green rug. It had a
red Hereford bull embroidered in the middle, and there were four
red cattle brands embroidered on the corners. I liked it here; there
was lots of stuff, and it had history. I picked up a copy of *Ford
Times* from a pile of magazines stacked at one end of the couch.
"A family magazine designed to attract all ages," it said on the
cover. I turned to an article on motor travel in New England and
began to read about where and what to eat along the road.

"Those boys will be in to eat pretty soon," my aunt said, rush-
ing in from the kitchen with an armload of things for the table.

"Come peel these spuds and visit with me."

"Where've you been all week? I thought you were only going
up there for a couple of days." Nee-Stoh, or Sis, as she was usually
called, had the same idea of visiting as my grandmother. She
talked nonstop and I listened.

I sat on an upside down bucket in the old kitchen with its
green and tan enamel Monarch wood range, bottled gas fridge,
and lack of running water or electricity. I ran a sharp paring knife
around the big brown potatoes as my aunt talked. "Where's

Neil?" I said, dropping the last peeled potato into the pot beginning to boil on the stove. Neil, her biological son, was tall and good-looking, with a movie star smile and sense of humor to match.

"Over by the creek irrigating," she said. "He should be in anytime."

I went outside and looked across the flat toward the dikes surrounding a second cutting of alfalfa. I could see a figure shoveling mud onto a bright green plastic turnout. It was hot, and the mosquitoes were beginning to swarm over the standing water.

The figure straightened and began slogging along a small ditch toward the house. It was Neil, wearing rubber boots, heavy overalls, a Levi coat over a long-sleeved shirt, gloves, and a handkerchief hanging out the back of his straw hat to protect his neck. He waved his free hand in front of his face constantly to clear enough mosquitoes out of the air to breathe.

Except for the mosquitoes, the scene was very beautiful as the sun went down in the west. I watched the shadows grow in the tree line along the creek and waited for Neil to make his way out of the water onto dry ground.

Sis's geese were at the edge of the meadow like some kind of welcoming party. There were eight or nine of them and they liked to roam around, feeding on grasshoppers and whatever else they ran across. Sis said they were good watchdogs and kept snakes away from the house.

As Neil approached the geese, a large gander lifted his wings and took a couple of steps sideways. I watched the gander work its wings some more, then suddenly stick its neck forward. Neil's hand shot down to his leg where the big goose had pinched him, and he rubbed it energetically as he stumbled back into the slack water. Then Neil's number-two shovel gleamed in the evening, a sign to geese that they had attacked the wrong man as he waded among them swinging wildly.

Sis had spotted the slaughter and was rapping loudly on a kitchen window. "Neil!" she shrieked, running out into the yard. "Neil, stop that! Neeiiilll!"

At least half the geese were dead when he stopped, hunched over, the shovel held in both hands like a weapon.

"Christ," Sis muttered when it was over, returning to her kitchen.

I was leaning against a corner of the house, clutching my stomach. Tears ran out the corners of my eyes as spasms of laughter rocked me.

Lame Bull

My aunt and I bickered when it was time for school to start in the fall. I hated having to go back to Shelby, and I don't think she liked it either but acted instead like it was just a pain to get my clothes together and make the long drive. My grandmother seemed to think she had earned the right not to have to be bothered and made herself scarce.

The trip was always gloomy for me, and I usually wondered what I would find when I got there. At the ranch things were predictable. In Shelby it seemed as though anything was liable to happen. My mother had taken up with a big Swede who was content to let her wait tables while he worked at being himself. I don't mean that to be as critical as it might sound—my mother was mean when she drank and she drank a little all the time. More than once I saw her give him withering treatment, and maybe he didn't have time for much else.

It seems like whatever had happened with my father and Leon soured my mother on relationships somehow, and she was tentative toward them after that. Which is not to say she didn't want a man around—she just didn't want things getting mucked up by having to fit into a traditional family structure, whatever that is.

From the vantage point of some years, I can understand better why my mother never compromised her freedom with another man, always keeping Dean at arm's length. She always claimed she didn't want any man to think he had the right to mess with Gary and me, but I think it was a more complicated thing than maybe even she knew. That and her and Dean's frequent habit of drinking and fighting were hard to deal with at a time when being like everyone else seemed the safest position to be in.

Dean and my mother have been together for nearly forty years now. I get along well with him, although I think we both understand the limited nature of our relationship. My father figures were among my mother's people, and they were a hard act to follow. When I think about Dean now, I realize I don't know much about him. He is a capable man, and I am sure there are reasons he had a hard time holding jobs, why he was never a husband and father to us, why he drank so much. I don't know his side of things, and that is probably not fair to him.

Around fourth grade I began to act out in response to some of the elements in my life and to my general resentment of not being allowed to stay at the ranch. I had a good buddy during this time, and we smoked, criss-crossed the town until late at night in all kinds of weather, began going out with girls, and stole everything that wasn't nailed down. We fought with the west-siders, hung out, played sports, and were cool in our own minds.

By sixth grade we were a little out of control. We drove his father's car to Cut Bank and back, bombed prom-goers from the top of the post office with popcorn boxes full of mud, and made detailed plans to break into the S & Q Hardware to steal bone-handled Crosman pellet guns.

Although I was still very angry at practically the very concept of Shelby, I began to think my antisocial behavior was getting dangerous. I worried about my mother and didn't want to get her in trouble. And I still remembered what had happened to Judy and didn't want to get sent away to Mooseheart.

Although I was on the verge anyway, the impetus to change my ways didn't come in the form of a supportive talk from my father or some other benevolent figure. I had never seen my father, and my mother's man wasn't about to take me and the rest of my family on.

I was drawing a horse on the pink Formica top of my desk while Albert Perrine conducted a math lecture. I could just as well have been on Mars when Perrine ripped me out of my desk, threw me against the wall, then jerked me out of the room and across the hall into the principal's office. "If you so much as move, I'll come back in here and paddle your butt," he said, slamming me into a hard wooden chair beside his desk.

My left arm hurt and I was scared shitless, but I kept thinking there were plenty of inattentive students in that classroom and for some reason Perrine had selected me to work out on. I didn't think for a minute he thought I was some kind of natural leader he could make the best example of. I thought he thought I had nobody to stick up for me, and I hated how his actions rekindled the feelings of powerlessness I associated with the time after Leon died and things really went to hell.

But that was enough for me. I didn't say another word or draw another picture that spring. I didn't do any more schoolwork either and began avoiding my friends. It wasn't long until school was out, and I concentrated on getting back to the ranch.

It was good to get back. The Milk River valley was bright and warm and there was time to study the pink Spanish-style church as we approached. My grandfather had no need of speed, preferring instead to lose himself behind the wheel in whatever ancient thoughts pleased him. Maybe he was reliving some part of his life that was important to him, or perhaps he could see beyond this life into the next; whatever it was he had seemed beyond speech as long as I could remember, and today he was content to let wind and tires talk for him while he concentrated on driving a steady thirty miles an hour. As we drew closer I could see the plaster saint was gone from its niche under the cross at the top of the front wall. A crack filled with gray cement snaked down the wall from the bottom of the niche.

Below the missing saint were two heavy wooden doors streaked at the top by weather. Above the doors was a large window that looked like half a wagon wheel with sunlight trapped between the spokes. In front of the building a big wooden gate stood ready to admit the dead; it had a cross affixed to its overhead beam like God's cattle brand. The grounds were fenced all the way around, with stout boxed corners and barbed wire stretched tight to steel posts in between. It was a good fence that looked as if it could keep the devil out, or keep souls in, I couldn't tell which.

The church didn't get used much anymore and might have been a total failure except for one thing. Sagebrush and cactus had been cleared to the east to make room for a cemetery. It was well kept in the way the dead are orderly; this was the place many women finally knew where their men were. The cruciform shapes of the wooden crosses were harsh in contrast to the puffs of cloud overhead; the sky was as blue as it would ever get.

The scene reminded me of my grandmother's story about her mother's bones. She said she wasn't sure it was right the way her mother had been laid to rest, so she made her brother Ed take her out to the mountains to the place the Gros Ventres used for burial, and she gathered up what bones she could find. She told me this story many times, and always I wanted to know what she did with the bones. She never told me, because every time she got to the part about Ed Shambo, it reminded her that he had been shot six times in front of the Hays Post Office by Willie Bradley. There was something about an impounded bull involved in the murder, and something about Ed Shambo having some kind of strange power over women.

I could never get it all straight, because my grandmother would become sharp and fierce like a hawk when she talked about it and rattle her pans with a vengeance. If I asked her again, she would change the subject and tell me a different story, like Ink'dome kills his wife. Ink'dome was crying for his wife, who had died, and a man came to him and asked him what was wrong.

When the stranger found out that Ink'dome's wife had died, he took a stick and shook it at his own wife, as if to strike her. On the fourth shake, he did strike her with the stick and she turned into two women. He gave one of the women to Ink'dome. After this, Ink'dome came upon a man whose wife had also died, and he repeated the trick he had been shown, doubling his wife and giving the grieving man one of the women. He was generous with his new-found power, and he gave a second man a new wife, then a third man. But, the fourth time, when he motioned three times, then struck his wife on the head, she fell dead, and he was alone again. The stories were a good diversion; I never found out what happened to my great-grandmother's bones.

I counted the white highway stripes going by slowly as we passed the church. Old U.S. 2 was narrow and patchy, widening to become well maintained and modern just past the west reservation line. The borrow pits on either side were deep and filled with brome and crested wheat grass planted by the highway department.

We turned onto the Hays road at Boo Kirkaldie's general store. This was the road where traveling salesmen were always picking up Angela Gone as she hitchhiked to Harlem. The thing was, she had been killed in a car wreck years ago at the spot they said they picked her up. She always asked to get out at Boo's, then disappeared. Boo's last name sounded like the song of a meadowlark. People said he wouldn't let his family drink Coke because he was financed by the Mormon Church.

The old man put in the clutch and roared the motor as we coasted through the turn and headed for Newtown. Once pointed straight, he jerked his foot off the pedal like it had burned him and let the car buck until it smoothed out on its own. I could see Snake Butte blue in the distance. It was long, like a snake, its east end a pile of rubble where the army had dynamited for rock to build Fort Peck dam. Old people said it was a tough job hauling that rock because it was full of rattlesnakes that fell down the windshields and tried to get into the cabs of the dump trucks. The burned-over Wolf mountains began further south, on the north side of the Missouri River. In between stood Three Buttes, an unconnected gallery captured in the middle.

My grandmother held a Kleenex to her nose as fine dust swirled up from the approach to Newtown. Many cars and pickup trucks made up the outer circle of a large encampment gathered for the Sun Dance, and we crunched over cactus and sagebrush to an empty space and parked. A few canvas tepees and many white-wall tents made up a smaller circle inside the vehicles. Inside all this was another circular enclosure made of cottonwoods and willows. First Sound's singers sat under a leafy canopy beating a large drum. I could barely see them inside, but their music seemed to come from out of the earth on its way to the sky.

We stopped at a tent where an old woman sat on a wooden kitchen chair tending a small wood stove. The stove had a single section of pipe sticking up crookedly from its back. The woman had long braids wound with red cloth. A leather thong bound her knee-high moccasins to her bowed legs, and she wore a wide leather belt around her dark-blue flowered dress. She poured coffee and Kool-Aid into enamel cups then signed "to open it up," and she and my grandmother started talking rapidly in Grovon. They talked too fast for me, but from what I could gather they had boarded together at Fort Shaw with a mean woman named

Mrs. Ring. My grandfather grunted occasionally for his part of the conversation as he and I looked off toward the sound of a tenor chant that had joined the beat of the big drum. The drone of the music seemed to join with the horizon of the evening sky, as if the health of the ear demanded a horizon.

After a while we got up and moved to the dance ground. First Sound's men were in full voice now. Most of them wore straw cowboy hats and dark glasses. First Sound held his left fist clenched to his ear as he sang with his head back, tilted up to the setting sun. The music was primal and endless, the pounding of the drum heavy like a heartbeat against the ears of the people settled into the branches of the circle. As part of the circle, the people were supported on both sides, connected all the way around, and in level contact with everyone else. No backs were turned. No one was ahead or behind. No one needed to worry about his or her place relative to other places. All places were equal, this circle part of a larger circle, and on and on, part of the whole circle of life. A man I knew as Glider from other dances began to move gracefully inside the enclosure, the first to go around. He was tall, with long black braids hanging down the front of his colorful print shirt. He also wore dark glasses and seemed to move forward and sideways all at once.

Others joined behind Glider, and as the procession moved ahead, a group of fancy dancers joined in to warm up, their ankle bells keeping time with the drum. Their costumes were elaborate, and occasionally one of them would bounce out alone, spinning circles within the larger movement, and then move back in line again to adjust a bustle or tighten a headpiece. A young man in full dress suddenly left the main body of dancers and began to dance tightly around the center pole. His long flat muscles seemed to lock and pop as he bobbed, spinning and looking behind as if to measure his movement.

We sat quiet on the margin of the celebration, our short hair and store-bought clothes stiff and unoriginal, but we smiled with everyone else when Big Belly Demarest took up a big chrome microphone and began to bray into it, "Let's give these singers and dancers a haaaand, these singers and dancers come from far awaaaay, and they're first on our agaaaanda tonight." Big Belly's Grovon broadening of vowels made the people laugh. He was a hang-around-the-fort man, and his words were out of place compared to Glider who was dancing alone with his large black eyes tilted back in total absorption.

I slept on the ground that night, not knowing when the drums stopped, not knowing when stories became dreams or dreams became stories. At some point I dreamed about the Dog-Dance. The people were traveling. They left a dog behind. The dog was smooth-haired but wore a shirt with feathers. The dog followed the trail of the camp. An old man went out on the hills. He saw something following the trail and wondered what it was. He went toward it to see. He saw that it was a dog and pitied it. Then the old man went to sleep by the dog. The dog knew that the old man pitied him, and in return he pitied the old man. In his sleep, the dog appeared to him and said, "I will give you a dance. It is to be called 'Shaggy Dog.'" Then he told the old man how they were to make the dance, what they were to wear, and how they were to dance. The dog gave him a whistle and a forked rattle and a headdress of owl feathers and a shirt covered with feathers. The old

49

man after a time gave these things to another, and so they were passed on to the present.

Summers always passed too quickly, but as I got older it was even worse. There was scarcely time to settle in before my Aunt Sis would start pestering me to get my clothes together. This particular fall there were four of us sophomores who dressed with the varsity, and we were down at the j.v. end of the locker room talking about how we hoped we didn't get killed during the game or atom-balmed after it. Atom balm was a red-hot analgesic that upperclassmen spread on your balls before throwing you in the shower. Water made the stuff ten times as hot.

LaBuff called the team for the pre-game meeting and we all assembled by his office.

"We can win this tonight and wrap up the whole thing if each and every one of you goes out there and hits somebody," he shouted. "I mean hit somebody and keep hitting somebody until it's all over; now let's go!"

The team roared in unison and headed for the door, jostling and slapping one another's helmets with open hands. My ears rang under the blows, and I felt like puking as the frozen gravel stung my cold feet. We jumped through a big paper-covered hoop and ran onto the field to warm up. It was very bright under the light flooding from the tall poles overhead. The crowd roared and I felt like pissing in my pants.

The teams were evenly matched and we went in at half time, the game tied six to six. The third quarter brought more of the same, with neither team making it much past mid-field. Both squads were beginning to tire, and we sophomores watched warily as players started finding excuses to get off the field. Then, sure enough, there was someone down near our bench, and La-Buff ran down the line of players and grabbed me.

"You're going in," he said, dragging me behind him. "You get that ball; you use some of that speed and *run,* goddammit." He was crazed, and his strong hand hurt my arm. "And I mean run *upfield,* not sideways. You're not worth a shit unless you're inside the ten-yard line. Tell Walker to go to two-minute offense as soon as Boling is off."

Boling was a scruffy-looking kid from the wrong side of the tracks, like me. He had never been anything but the butt of jokes about his overweight sister and his dad who was a janitor at the school, until one night LaBuff put him in to return a kickoff and he ran it back a hundred and five yards for a touchdown, then did it again in the same game.

I ran to the huddle and said, "Two-minute offense."

"What the hell do you think you're doing out here?" Walker replied.

"I'm in for Boling," I said.

"That's just great," he said angrily. "Okay, come on you guys. We're on the thirty; let's take it in."

I didn't have to do anything on the first two plays, so everything went okay. I kept looking over at the sideline to see if Boling was coming back in so I could get out from under the blinding, weird light.

As I moved around in a daze, a strange thing happened. It was as if someone had turned on a movie in my head, and I saw Melvina Horn's log cabin, sitting on its small knob west of the creek on the south edge of the valley where the ranch was. The sagebrush flat to the north toward the river had been cleared and planted in bluejoint, but Horn hadn't taken to farming very well. His claim to fame was the time he got drunk and bucked Melvina out of their wagon while crossing the creek.

Melvina Horn. Snake Woman. Worshiper of the sun. She stopped at the ranch once in a while to get an advance on her lease money. Nobody ever got out of the car when she came. The old lady and her people would just sit there until my grandfather went out; then they would wait while he looked in his book and wrote a check, if she had money coming. She wore her hair in braids and had rings on her fingers. She smiled and said very little. The younger ones wore fancy western clothes. My grandmother said they were good-looking people, but they drank too much.

"I wonder if I can get Jackson to help me stack that alfalfa in a couple weeks," my grandfather said one day.

"I think he got run off," my grandmother said. "He got Pearl in the family way and Melvina had to give her an abortion."

"You don't believe she can do all that stuff, do you?" he asked.

"She isn't called Snake Woman for nothing."

"I don't believe it," said my grandfather.

"What about Elmer Wing? She said she'd fix him for abusing Selena, and he's had the snakes ever since."

"That's because he drinks so much."

"Don't forget Clarence Mummy. When he went over there and gave Percy such an awful beating, she told him he would be sorry for coming in her house like that. And look what a horrible death he died."

My grandfather began to build a cigarette, rolling the thin paper around in his fingers while he sprinkled tobacco from a Prince

Albert can with his other hand. He didn't say anything more. He was big and red and slow-moving, but he was also thoughtful and capable of surprising action.

As the movie continued I remembered one day when the Jernigans from Saco were at the ranch. My grandfather ran cattle for them on shares, and once in awhile they would come to check on their stock and have an outing. They seemed sallow and fragile; he was very old and she was always worried about things like stepping in cowpies. They had a son who was a college student somewhere. He had come with them once, but the dog bit him and he never came back.

We were getting ready to brand some late calves and my grandmother's bay mare bucked her off by the corrals in front of the Jernigans. My grandfather was standing with a rope in his hands, about to get on his own horse, when the mare blew up. After she unloaded my grandmother she crowhopped a couple times and took off past my grandfather. In one motion he front-footed her with his rope, then straddled her as she struggled to get up. He freed her legs, and she started to buck again as soon as she regained her footing. He sat easily as she made a couple of jumps; then he took the end of the rope with the big Turk's head end on it and whipped her down both tender flanks. The knot made dander fly from her coat and she just kind of groaned and hunched up, splay-legged and trembling. As he stepped off, I noticed he hadn't even bothered to pick up the reins. I had once seen him whip a runaway team across an irrigation ditch full to the bank, and this seemed pretty tame in comparison. Mrs. Jernigan, however, had fled behind the pickup and was holding her hand to her mouth, her eyes wide with fright.

Catch Colt

The memory made me feel foolish, and I began to look at the game as Walker called the next play, a sweep around my end. I was supposed to block the outside linebacker, but when I got there he grabbed me and threw me out of the way. We kept going downfield and made it to their five-yard line with less than a minute to go. Walker called a timeout, then called for the sweep around my end again.

"Dammit, now everybody hit somebody," he panted.

I came off the ball as hard as I could and tore off downfield looking for somebody to block. There was a tall skinny guy just turning to go with the flow of players. He was trying to see who had the ball and never knew I was there until I cut his legs so that he nearly landed on his head.

I got up in time to see our halfback run into the end zone. The referee's arms shot straight up as the crowd roared. I didn't see the yellow flag until the line judge walked over to pick it up. He turned around and walked back toward the line of scrimmage, looking at our players. I watched him walk to a clear spot and chop at the back of his leg with his hand. I was praying by then.

"Clipping," he cried. "Number forty-four, offense."

I looked down at the two fours on my jersey, hoping they would go away. The gun went off and the game was over. As I walked toward the locker room a businessman in a trench coat and fur hat with a feather in it scurried after me, yelling something I couldn't understand. He was an insurance salesman in town, and had buttered me up after a track meet once. His gold fillings shone out of his purple face and his fur hat was crooked as we converged at the gate in the chain-link fence surrounding the field.

"What the hell's LaBuff teaching you, you Indian sonofa-bitch?" he screamed.

Our frozen breath collided and trailed off as I watched the man warily and thought of Snake Woman, and my grandfather, and of how good it felt to have the game over with, even the way it had turned out. I was afraid, but I was also brave, and I had dis-covered my fear, too, had a horizon.

Although I did fairly well once I got there, it's a wonder I ever made it into high school at all. For one thing, the light and space of Montana had zapped me in certain ways. In the presence of the Rocky Mountains I ignored Junior High Principal Lawrence D. McDermott's message that first day I stepped inside the door and he promised me a surprise. All I could see was the Big Sky and act-ing like a cowboy.

The relentless encroachment of modern life could hardly get a foothold in north Montana, a place where Indians and exiled Confederates conspired to resist becoming employees. Even winos had an attitude, and I guess it was hard to be submissive in the glow. Besides, I had learned some basic moves from Louis L'Amour and I was big on individuality.

First McDermott threatened me with some kind of vague retri-bution. Then I noticed school had turned into a place that priori-tized marching quietly to different rooms every hour over every-thing else. Nobody seemed very confident about what was going on, including the teachers, and we all reacted in different ways, me with a kind of hysterical humor, Arlene Zwinger by suddenly peeing what seemed like a gallon of splashing yellow urine onto the hardwood floor in social studies. Nobody said a word. It was us against them.

At a quarter to four in the afternoon classes ended and the more serious business of sports began. The emphasis in Shelby was such that everybody turned out, including kids who had no business doing so. Those who were not athletic got their first acquaintance with a certain reality, although it was also true that those who were athletic did too. The ultimate irony was that Shelby's athletic tradition was brought to it by an Indian coach from the Blackfeet Reservation forty miles to the west.

Jess LaBuff attended college on a football scholarship and graduated from Western Montana College, both accomplishments unheard of for Indians. Indians played basketball and stayed on the reservation. They didn't play football, and they never went to college. Stranger yet, he got a job in all-white Shelby and by 1955 his athletic teams were perennial champions and the town was becoming hooked on winning.

I don't know how he did it, but I am fairly sure one reason he succeeded had to be that he was too tough to be run out of town. The whole thing was extremely unlikely for the time, something made more clear by the fact that the end came when Jess was discovered dead drunk in the coach's office one morning when he didn't show up for his first hour history class.

In the meantime, however, Jess LaBuff brought passion and intelligence to a generation of prep athletes who were shaped by his influence. He ruled by discipline and intimidation, and if you survived you were made stronger, believed in yourself, and you loved LaBuff. If you failed you hated LaBuff; either way you were a changed person at the end.

Lame Bull

The LaBuff system began in seventh grade. Nobody was turned away from the football program, and there was a terrible seduction to unconditional acceptance and a uniform. It was only later that most players realized they were linemen.

That first year of football was more confusion than anything else. Gone were the carefree days of running with the ball or chasing after it. There were plays to be understood, techniques to be learned, and acceptance of the reality of contact. Eighth graders held most starting positions and seventh graders did a lot of incredibly detailed screwing around after fundamentals drills.

About all my class accomplished that fall was to learn things such as "Give 54 meant the 5 back through the 4 hole," and how it felt to tackle the four or five guys who were large men when they were fifteen. Tommy Jensen pissed in *his* pants during scrimmage one day, I made a couple of pretty good runs, and the season passed quickly. Shortly after football came basketball tryouts and on the Monday morning the roster was posted in the gym, I wasn't on it.

Basketball was the most prestigious schoolboy activity in town, and I had been a member of the starting five of one of the two grade schools. Usually, those two teams made up the seventh grade team and it was highly unusual that a starter from either team would not make the junior high team at all. McDermott and the basketball coach, Stump Littlefield, were standing by the roster the day it was posted. I searched the list frantically, then looked up as tears began to fill my eyes. Littlefield was fooling with his fingernails and McDermott was smiling broadly at me. Finally, I understood what he meant that first day of school when he said he had a surprise for me.

Catch Colt

That winter was horrible. I was so alienated that I withdrew into a laconic silence. It was the second time I had realized how badly screwed I was in some ways, and that all I could do was wait and hope things got better. One of the ways I coped was by retreating to the library. Reading helped a lot, but it didn't do much for my other study habits. Although I didn't realize it at the time, having to deal with being excluded was probably one of the best things that ever happened to me. The reading was very valuable and not only put me back in control of my own life but opened up worlds that would eventually make a real difference to me. And without a doubt, compared to Will James, Isaac Asimov, Robert Heinlein, and others, the warehousing and petty politics going on in the Shelby school system were as dry as dust.

Spring finally came and I went out for track to get out of last period study hall. The first thing we did was line up and race the length of the football field. I won by thirty yards. After that I wore the school colors and enjoyed athletic privileges.

On spring afternoons we matched ourselves against the other schools in the area. On those days I felt much more alive than in the stupefying routine of the classroom. Everything seemed in sharp focus as the crowds gathered to watch us gallop against one another in our newly maturing bodies.

Settling into the starting blocks was like being dipped in the brilliant energy of the sun. Waiting for the starter's pistol, I turned and burned in that energy, bathing in it and hating the power of it at the same time. The intensity of the start always made me forgetful, and I did not know the gun had gone off until I straightened fully from the crouch of the blocks at about the fifty-yard mark. There was a slight hunkering down into the sprint then, and a keening for the finish line that emanated from every cell in my body.

I always ran slightly beyond the finish, then turned back, unable to speak, vision still focused on that point in distance where endings may be found; turned back to dance on the body of the race. I broke all the conference sprint records for my class, and LaBuff took to showing up at track meets to watch me run. I ran without shoes, with adhesive tape wrapped around my socks. I ran alone; it was a pure thing, and I never cared much about teams after that.

Crying for Pity

Smith came to my aunt's house late one night. It must have been about eleven o'clock, and for him to be out at that time was very unusual.

"Buck, go for Doc Hamilton, quick," he said to my uncle in a panic-stricken voice. "Something's wrong with Jimmy."

Jimmy was his real grandson, the son of his son Jim. Jimmy's mother lived in town, and he had been staying with Smith and my grandmother for a few days. Jimmy and I must have been about ten or eleven years old, still the age of Thorns, although Jimmy might have been approaching the age of Bull Calves, which goes from about twelve to sixteen.

Catch Colt

My uncle got in his pickup and headed for town while my aunt
and I followed Smith home in the car.

"Holy fishhooks! Look at him go," my aunt said as we
watched Smith skid down the approach and bounce down the
gumbo tracks toward the river. "He left the gates open," she exclaimed, trying to keep up without running off the road herself.

When we got to my grandmother's the lights were on in the old
house and Smith was already inside. He was sitting at the kitchen
table kind of rocking back and forth, nervously clasping his hands
behind his head, then over one crossed knee, then back again. Every once in a while he would call out to my grandmother, who
was in the bedroom off the kitchen, and ask her what was going
on and if Jimmy was all right.

"He's quiet now. He's resting," she kept calling back. My aunt
had told me to stay with Smith while she went back in the bedroom, and that was the beginning of a duty I fulfilled for a long
time afterwards.

I sat still at the table with Smith, not saying anything, just kind
of keeping an eye on him, until my uncle and Doc Hamilton arrived. When they came in they went back to the bedroom, and I
carefully kept my gaze trained on nothing.

The doctor was a southern aristocrat who had somehow
landed in Dodson, Montana, with his wife Wilhelmtina and a
black slave named Robert. Robert had been a wedding present to
Miss Tina and did the heavy work around the Dodson Drugstore
where Doc Hamilton had his office and sold dry goods.

I borrowed a dime whenever we went into Dodson Drug and
bought a funny book with it. The book rack was in the back
where it was dark and Robert used to wait for me, his black skin

62

blending into shadows. He laughed like hell when I finally spotted the whites of his large eyes and told him I saw him. He used to run away once in a while, and there would be a big to do until he was found. He usually came back on his own, as if running away was just a bad habit he couldn't quite seem to forget.

Doc Hamilton came out of the bedroom way too quickly, removing his stethoscope and stuffing it in his scuffed bag as he emerged. He had suffered a stroke a number of years before, and he talked like a seal, barking out word sounds as his head bobbed up and down.

"He's gone, Smith," he said to my grandfather, recasting each word into three syllables as he worked to get them out.

My grandfather looked away and groaned, then sat quietly.

"I . . . I . . . I'm . . . sor . . . or . . . orry," Doc Hamilton croaked, putting on his black hat and coat as he turned to go.

Everyone gathered in the kitchen, pulling up chairs and making room around the table. My aunt brewed tea as my grandmother started to tell the story, describing how Jimmy had been playing in the house, then around bedtime began to complain of a headache.

She said he told her the pain was getting worse, so she wet a washrag to put on his head and went to lay down with him. When she called Smith just a few minutes later, Jimmy was foaming at the mouth and having convulsions.

She seemed to need to tell the story over and over again, emphasizing one part, then another, correcting herself in places until she was satisfied she had it right. Finally, she said Jimmy stiffened in her arms one last time as she tried to hold him down, then relaxed and was quiet. My grandmother knew he was dead when we got there, my aunt said later, and they were just cleaning him up and changing the bed while my grandfather and I sat in the kitchen.

It was chaotic most of the night. Somebody brought Jimmy's mother, Mary Jane, in, and she looked like she might up and die herself. At some point someone asked me if I wanted to go in the bedroom and see him. He looked like he was asleep, with the covers tucked under his chin. Later my grandmother told me how she had worked to close his eyes and smooth the grimace from his face with her hands.

As she talked, Smith sat staring into space. His eyes were dull with shock, and periodically a low groan rumbled from his chest. The hearse arrived from Malta a couple of hours later, and as the attendants wheeled the body past him he rose as if to stop them.

"Smith!" My aunt spoke sharply to him from across the room. "He's gone. Let him go." He sat down again. I had never seen him look weak or confused like that, and it made me want to cry.

On the way home my aunt told how Smith and my grandmother had lost a child, how his only son had been killed in a car crash a few years earlier, and how his first wife and another child had also died. When she finished she said bitterly, "Everything Smith has ever loved has died," and I realized she hated him for taking her mother away from her.

It was only three or four years later when Smith came late at night again. This time it was my grandmother. She had said earlier that day that her right eye was blurry, and by the time we got there she was in excruciating pain from the stroke.

They took her to the agency hospital that night, and I never saw her walk again. Smith was alone, so I stayed with him that summer, driving him back and forth from the hospital, then later the rest home in Harlem, and doing the chores. It was pretty good duty compared to working in the hayfields, but after awhile the other boys started calling me Smith's nigger.

I didn't mind. The house was full of books and magazines, and not only did I get to drive around in Smith's new car, but he didn't care if I read all day and all night, too. I read three or four years worth of *Outdoor Life* and *Sports Afield,* coming to know writers like Ted Trueblood and Jack Connors as if they were members of my own family. Later, when I took a job in Idaho, locals were amused at my extensive but thirty-year-old knowledge of the Snake River area gained from those two outdoor magazines.

By summer's end it had been decided that another of my aunts, Jackie, who also lived in Shelby, would care for my grandmother, so Smith went with me when I returned for my freshman year in high school. High school in Shelby was good. I had some luck at sports, surprised everyone including myself by getting back on the academic honor roll during my junior and senior years, and had a lot of fun.

Although my childhood friend Denny and I were always a little more serious than some of the other guys we ran around with, we managed to whoop it up once in a while, usually in the off-season between sports.

One spring evening we were dragging Main in Denny's '57 Chevy. Bob Olson was driving, and we were in the back drinking beer. Just past Main Street somebody threw an empty can out of the car toward the railroad tracks and the town cop spotted it. As soon as Olson saw the flashing lights of the police car, he romped on it and away we went.

We went south past the junior high, turned east past the courthouse, turned north again, and flew back across Main Street at eighty miles an hour headed toward the interstate and Canada. The road took us along the eastern edge of Shelby's north side, where Denny and I both lived.

As luck would have it, Denny's mother was putting the cat out just in time to see us roar by, maintaining a respectable lead on the police car in hot pursuit behind us. The police car was no match for the souped-up Chevy, and we easily outran it on the gravel roads north of town.

We did not, however, outrun Denny's mother, Mabel. When he walked in the back door a few hours later, she was waiting up for him. "What have you been up to this evening?" she said, concealing her wrath. "Oh, nothing much," he replied, and the shit hit the fan.

My grandfather and I also remained companions, driving around on Sundays, visiting his brother in Fairfield, occasionally driving to Harlem so he could do business at the bank.

Our roles gradually reversed, and by the time I was a senior in high school I cared for him like a child. When he died, he gave me the car in which we had traveled so much. It had 13,000 miles on it, and he and I had driven all but a few of those miles together.

I had a good job so I decided to stay in Shelby the summer after I graduated from high school. It was the first summer in my life I didn't go back to the ranch, but I wanted to go to college and thought I needed to earn more money than I could bucking bales.

Crying for Pity

A couple of weeks after school got out, my Aunt Sis showed up on a Friday afternoon and said she had to go to an Intertribal Policy Board meeting in Billings and wanted me to drive her. I was lonesome for her, so I agreed to do it with the understanding I would be back in time for work Monday.

Billings was farther than I thought, but after a long day of driving we got there and checked into the Lincoln Hotel downtown. I ended up going to most of the meetings, which were pretty boring until the afternoon of the last day. I was sitting in a metal folding chair trying to stay awake when a man stepped up to the podium and introduced himself as Robert Yellowtail Jr.

He spoke with words and signs at the same time, using both in ways I had never heard or seen. He started talking about the history of the northern tribes, describing who they were and how they saw things. He reminded the audience how important the earth and all the things of the earth were, and of the value of family and community. He ended by expressing sorrow at the way things were, then predicted they would be put right again in time.

By the time he finished I was sitting up straight in my chair, wide awake, savoring the way he said things. I know now his words were part of a song echoing through hundreds of years, establishing an "I" as "we" in the Indian experience, speaking for the community on many essential issues. It is not often we experience magic, but we know it when it happens. Magic happened that day. I have never forgotten it and have tried often to paint in broad strokes with language like Robert Yellowtail.

One thing led to another and I didn't get back to Shelby for almost two weeks. I figured rightly I had lost my job but went back to get my work boots so I could start swamping bales for Wink.

He found out I was home a couple of days after my aunt and I got back from Billings and by the next day had rounded up another hay truck for me to load and drive. My aunt was happy then. She thought I should be at the ranch and getting me to drive her to the meeting was how she accomplished it.

At the end of August I left for Billings again with my two other running partners from high school, Russ and Pete Nasset, this time to attend Eastern Montana College. Pete was a year older and had been to Eastern the year before, so he told Russ and me how to fill out financial aid forms and when to show up.

It was the fall of 1967, and we lived in Rimrock Hall with the largest freshman class in Eastern's history. The second night we were there we noticed a lot of activity outside the dorm and went to check it out. There was a large crowd milling around, and somebody told us the cops had been called to break up a panty raid on the girl's dorm next door.

The authorities were there in force, but there must have been five hundred students opposing them. A large uniformed man leaned over the top of his car with a bullhorn and said, "You are ordered to disperse and leave the area immediately."

Hundreds of voices replied in unison, "FUCK YOU," and the entire crowd spontaneously sat down. It was the kind of thing I had previously only seen from afar on television.

Nothing happened for the next fifteen or twenty minutes; then a chorus of boos erupted from the students. One of the crazy men from Butte, who was a campus football hero, was being led from the girl's dormitory in handcuffs. He was smiling happily, a pair of yellow panties around his neck. The crowd roared its disapproval as he was placed in the back seat of a squad car, and the firemen at the scene readied their hoses.

There was no further action taken, however, and after a few minutes the perpetrator was driven slowly away. We disbanded, feeling closer to large groups of baby boomers protesting various issues across the nation. It was a heady thing to be part of such large numbers at that time.

In addition, there were classes to attend, parties, football games, and students to meet from all over the country. So much was going on all the time that it seemed as if about all I could do was grab hold of the coattails and hang on.

Drugs like LSD and marijuana were available, but most of my friends had been raised around booze-fighters and drinking was what we did, although alcohol was bad enough. Pete and I got all drunked up on lime vodka in the dorm one night and ended up being hauled before the student disciplinary committee.

I think in many ways Pete's was the best mind of my generation. Big, handsome, a good athlete, he was also very precocious in a way that manifested itself in open rebellion in his early adult years. We were alike in our rebelliousness at times, although his was more a result of seeing through things while mine was the frustration of not being able to see through things.

We made an interesting pair, especially during those years we both drank heavily. We hung out a lot, shared many of the same intellectual interests, and had a habit of fighting one another when there was nobody else around.

The night we got nabbed at Eastern was very typical. Pete was always finding new situations, new interests, new people, and in this case he had made friends with a Filipino-American guy who was a very talented artist. We went to the guy's room and watched him paint his final class project, a giant impressionist bumble-bee, and drank lime vodka until we could scarcely see.

When we left, I went into the bathroom down the hall and told Pete to wait for me. Moments later I could hear him carrying on and an argument of some kind picking up speed. When I came out Pete was surrounded by resident assistants, who were responsible for keeping the peace in the dorms. He was insulting them roundly, and I did not hesitate in joining him.

The rest of the school year passed uneventfully except that I got busted off the track team for letting my grade point average drop below C. I was angry at myself for letting my grades slip, but things began to look up again when I got a summer job with the highway department in Shelby. Mom and Dean had moved to Helena, so I rented an apartment close to my grandparents. Gary hated Helena and came to live with me as soon as I had a place.

We had a good summer. I kept my nose to the grindstone and concentrated on saving money. Gary got to be with his friends, and, except for demolishing one stall of Albert Carter's car wash with my '58 Pontiac, pretty much behaved himself, too.

We went over to my Aunt Jackie's on Sundays to visit and take Smith for a ride. My grandmother was frail and had shrunk to about sixty pounds, but she was alert and loved to watch professional wrestling and order the Popiel Pocket Fisherman, Ronco's Veg-A-Matic, Ginsu knives, and other television products during commercials to give as Christmas presents.

My grandfather wasn't doing as well. His complexion was turning gray, and I had to watch him carefully as he walked even the short distances to and from the car. He no longer liked to go

anywhere far. He had stopped wanting to eat in restaurants after
he fell in the Capitol Cafe in Cut Bank and I had to grab him under the arms from the back and lift him up.

Pete and Russ switched to the university at Missoula that fall, but
I returned to Billings. Lenny Hill and I and a couple of other guys
lashed up together and rented a house on Avenue C. I kept my
grades up just enough to stay in school, devoting most of my time
to working as a mechanic at the Division Street Standard station.
I still identified strongly with my family and to me that required
working with my hands.

By Christmas we were all about burned out with fast living.
We worked all day and partied all night, every night, and after
four months of little sleep life began to seem a little shrill. Then in
about a week's time a number of things happened that caused us
all to change directions. Somebody left the heat off during a cold
snap and the water pipes broke in our house. The crawl space
filled with water, then the water froze and broke the house in half.
A couple of days later my girlfriend from Shelby called and told
me she was pregnant. The next morning my mother called and
told me Smith had died.

Sally and I were very much alike in certain respects. Our folks
worked hard and played hard, and we both just naturally pitched
in and helped with younger brothers, household chores, and more
or less took care of ourselves in the process. We were young, but
being a couple suited us in many ways. When she told me she was
pregnant, I never thought to do anything but return to Shelby and
get married.

I was on my way out of Billings by noon. I gave Darlene Allen my '58 Pontiac, put a thermostat in the Modified Production drag car I had built that fall, and headed north on racing slicks into a driving snowstorm.

The old man was still heavy when we packed him to the grave Neil had dug in the frozen earth with a spud bar and number-two shovel. We laid him next to Jimmy O'Bryan and then waited around for everyone to leave. We filled the grave when they were gone, stripping down to our white shirts. We were all there— Neil, Wink, Skip, Buck, and I.

I stayed with Neil until spring. He had bought my grandparent's place and it was comfortable there. I told everybody it would be hard to start my car until the weather warmed up because of its high compression, and that seemed like a good enough excuse. Sally wrote after a while and said she couldn't understand why I would go somewhere to do a simple task and stay there the rest of the winter. We were similar in many ways, but my Indian background was not one of them.

My grandmother started talking about death as soon as I got back to Shelby. I went over there the day after I got into town, knocked on the door, and waited. There was still dirty snow in the corners of the yard, but it was sunny and warm.

"Oh, it's you!" my Aunt Jackie said. "We heard you were on your way." She always seemed glad to see me, but I think it bothered her that my grandmother bought me things.

We walked across the living room then through the small central kitchen to the bedroom where my grandmother spent most of her time. She was lying in her hospital bed with the head elevated.

There was a triangular metal bar suspended above her and she had a Kleenex stuffed in the collar of her dressing gown.

Smith's bed was gone, and my grandmother's had been moved to the middle of the room. She seemed glad to see me and wanted to know everything that had happened since we talked last. I spent a lot of time in a chair at her bedside those years she was an invalid, and that was how it usually went. I would tell her what was going on in my life, then ask her questions about things she knew.

After we caught up on the news she wanted to hear about Smith's funeral. She dabbed at her eyes with the Kleenex as I told her about it, then said in her faint voice, "I'm going to die pretty soon, too."

I told her I didn't think that would happen for a long time, but she didn't seem convinced. After a while longer she started to talk about Smith again. She told how one time he got discouraged with ranching and leased out their place. They went to work for somebody else, she said, but after a couple of years returned home and worked for themselves again.

Later she told me about the last days he was there. She said he had been having dizzy spells and not feeling good. Finally one night he got real sick and Jackie called the ambulance. My grandmother told me how Smith said to her in sign language, "I'll go first and you come after," as the attendants wheeled him out of their room for the last time.

The story was heartbreaking, and I remembered it later when my mother told about sitting with Smith in the hospital as he lay dying. She said she held his hand and toward the end he smiled at her and said, "We did some cowboying, didn't we."

Catch Colt

All that afternoon my grandmother kept bringing up the subject of death, and I listened as best I could, just letting her say what she wanted. Later, as I started getting ready to go, she pointed up at the ceiling of her room and said, "Oh my, look at the ducks!"

Vision Quest

Sally and I were married that summer, and I decided to go back to school in Havre, at Northern Montana College. I had left Eastern without withdrawing and got a bunch of F's that reduced my grade point average to 1.13, so I really had to knuckle down. My daughter Lorna was born that fall and with taking care of her, studying, and working as a clerk for the Indian Health Service, there wasn't much time for anything else and I didn't go anywhere for months. In fact, the economic struggle that finally did Sally and me in had begun in earnest. I heard my grandmother wasn't doing very well, but I was shocked when my aunt called and left word she had died.

Catch Colt

The funeral was in Shelby, at the same place Leon's had been held some fifteen years earlier. They had put way too much red coloring on her face and she looked like hell. It bothered me that they didn't take her home, although my Aunt Jackie kept insisting that was what she wanted. I still didn't care much for Shelby and didn't want her there, so everything seemed out of place. I got drunk and cried in front of my mother and a couple of other people afterward, and the whole thing put me into a bad mood I couldn't seem to shake.

I tried to get over the grief, but it just got worse. I couldn't seem to concentrate on schoolwork or anything else. After a couple of months I began a course of action I didn't understand until years later when I began to read how the older Grovons organized their lives.

Without really knowing what I was doing, I began a kind of self-styled vision quest. I didn't go to Snake Butte as the old ones had done, but I put aside everything that was important to me and wandered around the northwest by myself for nearly a year.

I went to Seattle first, where I was born, then down to Eugene, Oregon, where Russ was living. Quite a few people I knew had gathered around the Indian Studies program at the University of Montana in Missoula, so I stayed there for three or four months before making my way back to the ranch.

"Oh, it's you," my Aunt Sis said when I knocked on the door late one night. "You have to sleep with Buck. Beatrice and them are here from Seattle."

And that was all that was ever said until my aunt told me about a week later, "Neil said to take his pickup and go get Sally and Lorna in Shelby. They're waiting for you." And they were.

The process didn't stop there, however. As I write this nearly twenty years have passed, and I am just beginning to get the sense that my particular quest is nearly over. I think there are at least a couple of reasons it has taken so long. First, memory of the vision quest is very faint at Fort Belknap, and achieving self-insight is a very difficult thing.

In addition, at the time I was reading a number of writers who believed in sacrificing a stable emotional life, sanity, and sometimes even life itself in order to get a glimpse of what lies "behind the veil of civilization." The social alienation that Melville, Conrad, Faulkner, Woolf, Hemingway, and others achieved as part of their own vision quests exacted a high price—they all flirted with despair, madness, and death over long periods of time in order to see their own heart of darkness.

As a result of having lost touch with the vision quest as well as not having a clear understanding about the influence of the reading I was doing, I think my behavior at that time was viewed by my family, and to a certain degree by myself, as a little crazy. Certainly the months following my grandmother's death were perceived that way, rather than something expected and necessary, as among older tribal people.

At any rate, my search allowed me to step back from outside influences and take a deeper look at what was happening around me. By doing that I was able to deal with my grandparents' deaths and return to a world comprised of the living and the dead.

I worked on a bridge crew outside Missoula that fall, then returned to Havre in the dead of winter determined to finish the one quarter I lacked to get my degree. It was snapping cold the night I got back in town, and I went knocking on doors looking for a way to make it happen. I visited three or four people that night, trailing my own frozen breath, until a professor named Frank Neisius offered to put me up for a while and saved my bacon.

I graduated from college that May, the first in my family to do so. My mother, my Aunt Sis, and my adoptive aunt, Aggie Adams, came to graduation. There they were, two Otter Robe women and the granddaughter of Heavy Brockie, like they had always been. There were no men from my family present that day, and that, too, was as it had always been.

Although I had always been a reader, getting the hang of college work had been a difficult thing to do. On my part, main force and enthusiasm seemed to work best. The one thing the college seemed able to do effectively was to be supportive while I figured things out for myself.

Grateful as I am, the institutions I attended contained few individuals who were willing to provide the kind of support necessary to be genuinely helpful to a student. In many cases that was because the student-instructor ratio simply did not allow for it.

The unfortunate state of education became more apparent when I took a high school teaching job the fall after I graduated. The salary was appallingly low, and I soon realized that when my student loans came due I would not be able to pay them and live too.

Not long after that I heard some of the men around the ranch talking about somebody who had been "sold out" by the bank. The individual and his family had moved to Billings, where he had gotten a job teaching. The men were talking about what a "scissorbill" the guy was, and that it was fitting he should be a teacher because those who couldn't do, taught.

I suddenly felt myself to be held in low regard by virtually everyone. I recalled other things I had heard and it seemed students, administrators, my own family, and the lowliest of unskilled workers clearly held teachers in contempt. Once again I felt myself a marginalized person on the edge of yet another kind of existence.

High school teaching was so discouraging I immediately began making plans to do something—anything—else. Northern had a Master's program in what they called Career Guidance, so I resigned my teaching position, enrolled for the next fall quarter, and went home to work at the ranch for the summer.

We didn't realize it quite yet, but the summer of 1973 was very close to the end of ranching as my family had come to know it. Within two years Neil and I realized the line of credit my uncle had worked so hard to establish was no more than a method for the orderly transfer of our land to the bank, and we sold our cattle. Skip was dead of kidney failure by 1978, and by 1980 Wink and my uncle were out of the cattle business also.

That summer was a good one. Everyone was busy working cattle, then putting up hay, and Neil and I leveled a bunch of land for Louie Gilbert with a J619 Cat scraper he had leased. Neil amazed me with his willingness to share what he had with me. He was by then a self-taught civil engineer and taught me to operate the scraper while paying me good wages to do it.

In fact, Neil was more or less the reason I got into the bar business. When summer was over I returned to Havre and started the Master's program at Northern. A few weeks later I was visiting with Bill Thackeray, one of the truly excellent professors at Northern, and he asked me if I wanted to buy a bar.

Catch Colt

Bill's brother had bought this little place up the Hi-Line for his father-in-law, one-eyed Johnny Hennesey, who soon revealed himself to be a serious booze-fighter. Bill said under the circumstances his brother was willing to sell for $5,500, including two buildings, fixtures, equipment, and an 80 ft. by 120 ft. lot in Joplin, Montana. There was no stock because Johnny had drunk it all up.

We drove up there the next day and the place captured my imagination. I told Neil about it and he gave me $1,500 "back wages" for the down payment. I had never been behind a bar in my life, but for some strange reason the business did well.

In the spring a man I had come to know as a morning customer came into the bar purple and sweating. It was about nine o'clock, and a four-day wind was depositing dirt and debris on the remaining snowdrifts. I had started swamping the bar with a scoop shovel, and Goldberg's heavy boots caked with prairie soil were starting the mud battle all over again.

Goldberg's father arrived with the second wave of settlers to the Montana Hi-Line area along U.S. Highway 2, about 1910. By then the choice spots by streams and roadways had been taken, and he was forced to homestead further north on a small flat spot in the middle of nowhere.

He surrounded his house with tough Caragana hedges and put lawn chairs in his yard of close-cropped prairie grass, but they were not nearly enough to hold back the emptiness. Goldberg's father died of loneliness, and Goldberg bought a fifth of whiskey and two six-packs of beer from me every Monday morning to help fight the incessant wind and intrusive sky. I knew he made the same purchase from at least two other bars on different days of the week.

After Goldberg left, things were quiet again and I returned to sizing up my own life as I mopped. I had bought into a different world for five thousand dollars. It was different because it was rich, part of what was called the Golden Triangle, an affluent wheat farming region that included eight small towns along a fifty-mile stretch of the old Minneapolis, Saint Paul and Manitoba Railway, now known as the Burlington Northern. It was rich because the land produced large quantities of hard red winter wheat, land that had been stolen from the Gros Ventre people just a few years before.

Over the winter I got acquainted with people pretty well. At first I don't think the community knew what to think of me, but when they realized I was a hard worker and shot a pretty good game of pool, they began to come around.

As the snow melted, I could see the old wood-and-tin joint had become a hangout for farmers resonating to a new member of their community, a breed kid who mimicked the things necessary to live there and to whom they had decided to offer friendship.

It was a strange dance that took place in a grimy honky-tonk that once housed a Chinchilla ranch, and where the floor flexed noticeably under profitable Saturday night crowds.

At the Rocky Mountains the Milk River arcs north past Saint Mary into Alberta. It re-enters the United States somewhere north of Hingham, leaving a deep cut in the ancient sea bed over which it flows. In the winter of 1924 over fifty men left Joe Johnson's saloon in Hingham, headed toward the Milk River to hunt jackrabbits. Such mass hunts were a popular activity for a number of years until there was nothing left to shoot. Snoose Gilbertson took a load of bird shot in his backside later that afternoon, and many rabbits were slaughtered by drunk farmers tear-assing through the sagebrush on tractors and flivvers of all kinds.

Charlie the Fox and I locked the doors to the Palace Bar at two o'clock and headed north past the old rabbit-hunting grounds toward the river breaks. There was a hard frost already, and we planned to be at Blacktail Coulee at daylight. We had started drinking the afternoon before at the dumpground, a long trench with sloping ends dozed in the earth at the east end of town. Alvin had borrowed Charlie's pickup to haul his garbage, and we were keeping an eye on him to see that he didn't tear it up.

Alvin's father had been killed in a car wreck a few years earlier, and his grandfather had gradually put him in charge of the family farm. Since becoming a proprietor he had also become a nuisance. He was all business, and it seemed like the only time we saw him was when he wanted something.

Charlie had a well-preserved old pickup he kept around for a spare, and Alvin had showed up earlier in the day demanding to use it since all his rigs were too busy to use for hauling garbage. Reverse gear was located down and to the left in the old Chevrolet, and it was easy to mistake it for second. Alvin was backed up to the north end of the trench when we got there and looked as if he was just getting ready to leave.

"That sonofabitch has gone crazy," Charlie said. "I never seen anything like it."

"Maybe he'll lighten up when he gets that grain hauled," I

said. "He had me up at six in the morning all last week after I tended bar until two."

"His old man was an asshole," Charlie said, "and I believe this one is going to be just like him."

"Well, he's going to buy us some beers this afternoon whether he knows it or not," I said.

"Damn right," the Fox said.

We pulled up to the opposite end of the dump and stopped, watching as Alvin jumped into the cab of the pickup and slammed the door. As he bent down to start the motor, the pickup started rolling down the incline into the trench, which was filled with garbage and burning with a black, oily smoke. Alvin roared the motor loudly, dumped the clutch, and shot backward down the slope into the fiery refuse.

"Goddamn," Charlie the Fox yelled, "Goddamn." He jerked open the door of the vehicle we were in, jumped out, and raced down the trench toward Alvin. I held the steering wheel tightly, fighting for breath through convulsions of laughter as the two figures, shouting and waving wildly, manhandled the stricken vehicle up the incline.

I made Charlie tell me the story of chewing Alvin out about his pickup two or three times as we drove north. It was false dawn when we got to the shack at East Butte. The shack was ten-by-twelve, eight-and-a-half feet high at the front, six-and-a-half feet at the back, with a six-by-ten foot extension that served as the kitchen. The tar paper on the outside was in shreds, and some of the roof shingles were gone, revealing the rubberoid roofing underneath. Inside was a mouse-ravaged folding couch, a one-burner laundry stove, a makeshift table, one straight chair, and a small warped rocker. The interior had been sealed with resaw and felt paper.

The lady who owned the place was eighty-four years old and still drove out by herself from North Dakota every year to check on her homestead. She had given the key to Charlie so he could keep an eye on it. He was always collecting old people, and had three or four he looked out for.

We had pickled eggs and beer for breakfast, then swept the place out and locked up. "How'd you like to have been raised in this sonofabitch?" Charlie said as we bumped into each other in the semi-darkness.

At daylight the Milk River was a dark ribbon deep in the lightening land. On the other side was Canada, and from where we sat it was easy to see the different strata in the canyon wall that had been bared by the river as it cut downward.

The land was too rough to farm this far north, so ranchers used it for grazing. We had connections with a cattleman named Laageson, who allowed us to hunt coyotes and deer on his land in return for beer and news from town. By mid-morning we had a couple of fat muleys and headed for the old bachelor's house. He was gone when we got there, so we put some backstrap in his refrigerator and left the beer on the kitchen table.

"Well," Charlie said when we got back into the pickup, "why don't we head back south. We'll stop and see if the Hoots are lookin' for any fresh genes today."

"Not likely they'd want to breed a deaf Polack like you," I said.

"Better'n a blanket-ass like you," he replied, cracking two more cans of beer.

The Hutterite colony was laid out like the military barracks at the radar installation north of Havre. There were four or five long, low, one-story buildings used for living quarters, a shorter building in the middle where the people ate and had their school, and a number of well-tended metal buildings where produce, grain, and animals were kept.

In spite of the fact they were generally despised by their neighbors, who had been taught to hate their communal lifestyle, and who thought they were out to gobble up all the land they could get, the Hutterites were good farmers. We didn't give a shit about politics and enjoyed visiting them.

We drove into the yard and a stocky man in heavy shoes, black broadcloth pants, suspenders, and plaid shirt walked over to greet us.

"That's Jacob, the head hoot," Charlie said.

"Good afternoon, Charles," Jacob said. "We haven't seen you for a long time."

"Hello there, old friend. How is your crop this year?"

"Oh, most of it ran better than twenty-five bushels. And yours?"

"'Bout the same, I guess," Charlie replied.

A number of others had gathered around, and we talked farming. After a time Jacob said something in German, and the group began to disperse. A couple of older men hung back, and when the others were out of earshot, they told us to meet them down at the shop.

"Charlie, did you and your friend bring anything to drink?" a ferretlike man with no front teeth said.

"Better believe it, Speedy," Charlie said. "Right in that cooler there."

"Charlie, what is it that you need today?" Speedy asked, taking a long pull at the cold beer he had fished from the cooler. "I've got eggs and some nice fryers," Speedy continued.

"Tell you what, Speedy, you break out some of that dandelion wine, and we might take some of them birds off your hands. By the way, how about a good deal on a goose?"

"Sure, Charlie. Darius, go to the cellar and bring back a jug."

The wine was good, slightly sweet and surprisingly powerful. We passed the jug back and forth until it was half gone. Darius brought a bundle with a half-dozen dressed chickens and a good-sized goose wrapped up inside.

"Fifty a pound and the goose for eight dollars," he said.

"Jesus, Speedy. I'm not a rich man," the Fox began to haggle.

"Charles, Charles, these are the best we got. Safeway buys them for fifty-four a pound."

"Christ, Speedy. You got a birth certificate on any of these things? They look like they died of old age."

"Well, okay. Forty-eight on the chickens, but I must have eight dollars for the goose."

The Fox had played this game many times before and knew it was time to deal. "You got it, Speedy, old friend, if you'll throw in the rest of this dandelion paint remover."

"You know that's good wine."

We concluded the deal and drove out of the yard onto the high-grade gravel road for home. The sun was bright in the cool afternoon air. We drove slowly past East Butte, towering high in the middle of the flat plain, toward another night shift at the Palace Bar. We were both drunk as hell.

I listed the Palace with a realtor in the spring, just to see what would happen, and it sold immediately for quite a bit more than I paid for it. But that was far from the end of the story. After two more years of working in education, I was poor again and ready for a break, so I bought the place back.

Wallace Goodheart, an implement dealer from Havre, had bought the Palace from me to have somewhere to stash his girl-friend while he divorced his wife. He tore down the old buildings, built a new bar, and generally cleaned the place up. Two years later, when things had quieted down in Havre, he sold it back to me.

Joplin was the westernmost among Kremlin, Gildford, Hing-ham, Rudyard, Inverness, and Joplin. The towns were about ten miles from one another and would have made one nice small city, but they all liked their independence. Joplin's population was about two hundred, but many more people lived in a fifty-mile ra-dius. The Palace Bar had been a local joke in the past but began to surprise everyone by attracting the kind of crowds associated with a much larger place.

One night I rang up more than twelve hundred dollars tending bar by myself with two barmaids delivering drinks to tables. The crowd just kept getting bigger, and after a while I didn't have time to use the till and started throwing money in a cut-down card-board beer box.

It was in the fall. Harvest was over and the younger folks were getting ready to go back to school. I came on shift at six o'clock and started cleaning up the happy hour mess. Cards and chips from the Pan and Pitch tables had to be put away, there were coolers to be stocked, and the day shift cash register tape and till had to be changed.

By eight o'clock the day crowd was nearly gone and the night crowd began to filter in. Alvin and Kantorowicz were among the first to arrive, arranging themselves at the north end of the bar. Kantorowicz was a pest whose idea of conversation was to argue about the price of everything.

Ronny Brady came in smelling like pig shit as usual. Ronny was a sleeper and never lasted much past ten o'clock. He would come in, have a few drinks, then go to sleep on the bar with his head on his arms. Aside from the smell and taking up space he was no trouble, but there wasn't much money in it for me.

By nine things were starting to pick up pretty good. The barmaids both showed up on time, and I gave them each a twenty-dollar bank so they could make change. Alvin was hitting the Mai Tais pretty hard, and Kantorowicz had started up a steady bitching about the price of beef jerky.

It was after ten when somebody set off a firecracker under the pool table. The noise was deafening even over the noise of the crowd, but I was practically on a dead run behind the bar and didn't pay much attention. What was really worrying me was that it looked like I was going to run out of quarters, and I was trying to think of where I could get more.

About that time I began to notice a kind of gradual delamination caused by everyone getting drunk. It was the time of the night every bartender dreads unless he is drunk himself. Out of the corner of my eye I saw Alvin reach for his big Mai Tai glass and miss by a mile, sending it crashing to the floor. He stood up as if to take some kind of action, then put his hand to his mouth and puked through his fingers instead.

Some girl I didn't recognize was over by the dance floor crying hysterically. There was a small crowd gathered around her, trying to get her calmed down, and I could only wonder what had caused all that. Swede Johnson was sitting at the south end of the bar and had begun to look intently at some guy who kept bumping into him from the back. I knew it was only a matter of time before Swede cold-conked the guy if I didn't do something.

In the midst of all the chaos I heard a muffled whump followed by a bunch of confusion toward the back of the bar. I was serving drinks as fast as I could and trying to see what was going on when LeeAnn Petersen stomped up to me crying and shrieked, "What kind of a damned looney-bin are you running here anyway!"

She turned and stormed off before I could reply, and I could see her hair was wet in back and there was a piece of toilet paper stuck to her blouse. She always kept herself all fixed up and I wondered what was going on.

Charlie the Fox shouldered his way through the crowd and said, "You better go take a look at the men's can. I'll tend bar for a while."

When I got back there, a large crowd was taking turns looking at the ruined bathroom. The stool had been blown off the floor, and the walls, ceiling, and door punctured by porcelain shrapnel. Water was spraying from the remains of the toilet tank hanging crookedly from the wall, so I shut off the valve underneath.

"What in the hell," I thought to myself, then remembered the firecracker that had gone off earlier. Immediately, I knew what had happened. Whoever had the fireworks had thrown an M-80 in the toilet bowl, closed the lid, and gotten the hell out of there.

It was an old trick. An M-80 is equivalent to a quarter-stick of dynamite, and the fuse will burn under water. There is just enough time to get out and close the door before the explosion destroys the bathroom.

Later I found out what had happened to LeeAnn. The men's and women's bathrooms were back to back, with a plumbing wall in between. That meant that the fixtures in both bathrooms shared common water lines and drains. The explosion blew the water out of both stools in the women's bathroom. LeeAnn was sitting on one of the stools and next to the other when it went off.

Although the money was good and some of the friends I made in Joplin were everything a man could want, there was something about the place that bothered me. I couldn't help thinking that something wasn't quite right, and after a while I knew what it was. These were the people who had weaseled in on the land after it had been stolen from the Gros Ventres.

After I scrapped with a couple of them when I first got to town, we came to a working arrangement, but they still had a healthy prejudice against Indians. On some level that pissed me off, and I resisted thinking of Joplin as home, setting it up in my mind as something to be exploited back. And that is exactly what I did. I worked the place for all it was worth and after two years sold out again and bought practically an entire block of downtown Havre, complete with the Montana Bar.

Going back to Havre was like going back to the Indian wars.

"Fuck, fight, or hold the light" was a saying around Havre that pretty much characterized my time in the bar business there. I had figured out only one reason to be in the bar business and that was to make money. I went at it with a vengeance.

But there were other reasons for my approach, I think, an approach that kind of precluded joining the Jaycees and the Lion's Club. My great-grandfather, Louis Chambeaux, and other shirt-tail relatives like Gus DeCelles had practically founded Havre, and yet the town treated Indians like dirt.

For the first time in my life, however, I had serious money, which translated into power, and I wanted to see if things could be different. It had always been clear to me how Havre felt about Indians, and about me, so I didn't think there was any reason to waste time on niceties. Montana had a legal loophole called "the swinging door provision" for food and beverage businesses that allowed for a number of operations to be run under one liquor license as long as there was "a swinging door" between them.

I brought in a couple of buddies from Joplin and in six months had three bars, two restaurants, a poker room, a cabinet shop, and four small apartments going in the Montana Bar building. Business took off like a rocket, and soon we were so busy there was no time to pay any attention to anything but what had to be done at the moment. It was like the Palace Bar times ten, with a back-breaking workload, more than forty employees, and a clientele that was not nearly as nice as the folks further up the Hi-Line.

It wasn't too long before the competition in town complained that the Montana Bar corner was "just too wild," and something had to be done. I replied that I thought that was kind of like handing out speeding tickets at the Indy 500, and that only made them angrier.

Fairly early on, a big old kid named Jack Claymore came in to see who was going to run the place. It's an old scenario in the Hi-Line bar business, and if the owner gets bluffed, whoever bluffs him pretty much has the run of the place. It was pretty clear right away what was going to happen, so I told Claymore I would call somebody to tend bar for me, and as soon as he got there we would go outside and settle it.

There is no way to feel more alive than being trapped behind a bar waiting for some pathological asshole to see if he can kick the shit out of you. I got a bottle of Peppermint Schnapps down and started sipping to calm my nerves, then went back in the office and got a roll of nickels and put them in my back pocket under the bar towel I usually carried.

Ronnie Blakeslee finally showed up to tend bar, and we started for the door, me in front, Claymore behind me, and a crowd of delighted onlookers following him. The front door of the Montana Bar had a step down to the sidewalk, and you had to look down as you went out to see where you were going. I went out first, and when Claymore looked down, I drilled him under the left eye with the roll of coins I had put in my right fist.

Nickels flew everywhere and Claymore seemed surprised that I would do such a thing. While he was thinking I loaded up on my right foot and started throwing short left-right combinations, shuffling up closer to set up again after each one. I could see skin come off his nose and his left eye begin to close as the punches landed.

A couple of guys stepped in and broke it up as soon as they

saw their man was getting the worst of it, and both camps went to their fighters to talk. We milled around a little, and somebody offered to buy a drink. Claymore turned to go back in the bar, and I grabbed him around the neck from the back and threw him down on the sidewalk.

"Jesus Christ," I heard from the crowd. "That's not fair!"

"Just leave 'em go," somebody else said.

I jumped on top of Claymore and hit him a couple more times when he went down, then he started to get up. I weighed about a hundred and eighty-five pounds and was kneeling on his chest, and he was getting up. I put my left hand on his face, hooked my right arm through a car bumper, and tried to push him back down, but he still got up.

At that point I thought I had made a *big* mistake, but Claymore had been whipped by the first punch. His punches were slow and wild and the rest of the fight I just kept stepping inside and throwing six-inchers at his ribs. Suddenly, he took off running and it was over.

Claymore was big, and I was afraid of him, but I remembered the ancient cavernous civic center where the Catholic priest Emil Rouse coached the Optimist boxing team. He was a weird, boyish figure dressed in black who beat the shit out of you in sepia light, then made it seem like the greatest thing in the world.

I always remember how he started the training. Two lines facing each other across the width of the gym. Blow, parry, blow, parry, over and over again in slow motion. After a while the boxing became automatic, the blow and parry, then the counterblow, and you saw things differently from then on.

And always the lines facing each other, the form, was the important thing. Boxing taught me Christianity, I think, taught me suffering and pain are necessary things, and I was amazed how simple both were in the end. Then came the smoker at O'Toole's and the kid from Great Falls who hit so hard. And big Gene Arquette slugging it out with Poti Talaluto, a Hawaiian who smiled throughout the fight.

After that night we were known. And we saw things differently. Things were different. Things were different again, and the tricks I used on Claymore had been used on me by a skinny Indian kid from Browning after a high school dance one night when I was about fifteen years old. I was the light-heavyweight champion of the Montana Bar corner for about two years, and of the small accomplishments of my life, that probably gives me the most unholy pleasure.

As it turned out, Claymore was the least of my problems. The business was really on a roll, and some of the other bar owners had decided to do something about it. City inspectors of all kinds started showing up, followed by Internal Revenue Service agents demanding to see the books.

But those things really didn't matter. I had proved I could do this thing of work, money, and power, and that was the point. Once again I realized I was much more interested in finding out about this community than becoming a permanent part of it. One day Reuben Azure came in and started blowing off about how I was the best, how I was the toughest man in Havre. I had won a few fights, it was true, but I wasn't stupid enough to think for a skinny minute I was the toughest man in Havre. What I did think was that I was pretty sure Reuben's words meant there would be others coming to find out.

It wasn't long after that that Jack Claymore shot his wife, her boyfriend, and himself to death in a drunken rage. I thought for a couple of days about what he had done, added that to dealing with employees, taxes, insurance, and the million other things that went with being a proprietor, and decided to retire on my own before I was retired by someone else.

I locked up on a Saturday night, packed up my wife, daughter, and two new babies the next day, and headed for California, where I spent the winter.

Crazy Lodge

       I knew it was time for me to leave Montana, but not because I sensed things would go so badly with the economy there during the 1980s. My reasons had more to do with some bad habits. I drank too much, chased women, worked too hard, and I was arrogant.

       It was always a grinding struggle for Sally and me financially, except in the years I owned a bar, and a couple of times we came up short and had to rely on my family. After that I believed it was possible I would not be able to take care of myself and my family, and that caused me to overreact.

       I also had it in my head for the longest time that I wanted to make my life at the ranch. When ranching and my backup teaching career both turned out so bleakly I became driven by the idea of making enough money to be secure. I was able to do that in the bar business, but in so doing I came to realize that I had slighted my wife and children. I worked day and night, and when I was not working, I thought about work.

Realizing the strain I was putting on my marriage, I hedged against the possibility that Sally would leave me by spending time and money on other women. It is an old story that is hard to dress up, and there are no excuses for some of the things I did to achieve success.

There are also no excuses for the pressure monolithic capitalism places on individuals to make money at the expense of their individual identities, their families, and their communities, and I think that is worth mentioning as well.

I loved the freedom and independence of Montana, but I had gotten out of control with my pursuit of money and I didn't want to live the second part of my life the way I had lived the first part.

It took awhile to decompress after growing up in Montana, but the West Coast did a good job of exposing me to a different set of problems. In that region were many people, few jobs, and much less of the long-rider attitude common to the Big Sky country.

Instead of being motivated by well-defined codes of independence and self-sufficiency, the Californians I met seemed to look to advertising, the mass media, and politics for clues about what they should do. Few answers were to be found, however. The economic structure that had held up for so long there was giving way, and the only work I could find was another low-paying teaching job, so I decided to move on again.

Responding to a flyer seeking Indian graduate students, sent to me by a friend, I moved to Brookings, South Dakota, where I did a master's in English at South Dakota State. When I got there, I realized Brookings was only about twenty miles from Flandreau, South Dakota, where my aunts had attended Indian boarding school. I also realized my father lived less than a hundred miles away.

I was still pretty defensive in those days, not real sure if I was a cowboy or a schoolteacher, Indian or white, good or bad. One of the ways I coped was to tend bar, do my personality act, and adopt a casual and laconic attitude maintained by Windsor whiskey mixed with a little soda water.

South Dakota State's homecoming weekend is called Hobo Days, and there is a wonderful parade on Saturday. One of my drinking buddies and I crashed the 1981 parade in his Corvette. The car had signs on the doors advertising me as "Big Sid—English Teacher of the Century." The truth of the matter was that I was a lowly teaching assistant who had only been in town a couple of months.

When we turned from a sidestreet onto the main parade route, I saw a large contingent of English Department faculty standing on the corner right in front of us. As they read the signs, I saw mouths drop open, and people turn to each other and ask, "Who the hell is Big Sid?" I was full of Cinnamon Schnapps, throwing candy to children, and I didn't care.

It turned out that the English Department had a sense of humor and thought the incident was amusing. One of them, a former Marine Corps Major and Vietnam veteran named Charles L. Woodard, became a close friend who guided me through a master's thesis and taught me to believe that someone like me could live a life of the mind.

I was still skeptical about teaching but interested in a profession where I could do some good, so I applied to law schools in the spring of 1982. I was accepted by three or four and decided on the University of Minnesota, which had Native American law listed among its course offerings and was only 200 miles from Brookings. Sally and I packed up the kids and our meager belongings once again and headed further inland.

The first year was very difficult, as I have heard most law school programs are, but the time after that was good for us as a family. Sally worked full-time, so I took over many of the household and parenting duties. We jawboned our way into buying a house on Lake Nokomis in south Minneapolis, the kids did well in school, and we were quite happy until the job market reared its ugly head again.

The classrooms in the law school were built like small amphitheaters. Students sat in graduated rows facing the professor's desk in the pit at the bottom.

The Greeks were emulated further by what was referred to as the Socratic method of teaching. This meant that the professors never gave a straight answer to anything. You were supposed to figure things out for yourself.

Such a method might have worked if original thinking counted for anything. But it didn't. Only tested, accepted answers were appropriate, and it was disastrous to respond in any other way.

This made us cheap hustlers of upperclassmen, who knew the answers, and of professors who didn't change their tests very often.

Each student's name was listed on a seating chart that guaranteed they would be called on to answer questions in class a certain number of times during the semester. As soon as this became apparent, a number of us moved to empty seats in the higher rows and kept quiet when we were called on. Others talked whether they were called on or not.

Attendance was not required, and blind grading that supposedly ensured the professor didn't know who had written examinations was also policy, so lurking in class worked out quite well. In fact, Paul Lazear graduated magna cum laude after living in New York City throughout law school, returning only for examinations.

The lighting in the room was very bright. It heightened the ability of the grass-green carpet and upholstery to irritate the senses. It was also two or three degrees too cold as I sat in the upper deck with a gunner bingo card, and as those who always seemed to feel the need to speak asserted themselves, I placed an X on the squares containing their names.

Gunner bingo was one of Todd's promotions. He made up the cards and sold them for five bucks apiece to selected players, retaining what he claimed was a small handling fee for himself. Today's pot was slightly over thirty dollars, a nice piece of change for law students who were broke.

A guy Todd had nicknamed Free Spot was talking, as usual. He spoke rapidly, with a big voice. It was hard to tell if he was as smart as he sounded. I marked Free Spot in the middle of my card and noted that I was only two names short of a diagonal bingo.

Hawkins was one of my remaining names. She was outspoken, tending toward evangelism. She had tried to make her points a couple of times by referring to the Bible and had been quickly reminded that there was no connection between the Good Book and the Law. I was pretty sure I could count on her to fill a space.

The legal discussion going on was a powerful anesthetic. I tried to fight off drowsiness by thinking about Robin Winters, a barmaid at Bullwinkle's Saloon. I savored the images in my mind one by one, trying to analyze what it was about her that called up such powerful emotions in me.

Maybe it was her thick, honey-blonde hair. I had read somewhere that thick hair was a sign of fertility. Robin's hair was brown and gold all at once, and grew wildly down her neck like a mane. I slipped further into the trance and thought about the hair between her legs.

I made it thick and springy, a rich triangle of curls within curls that curved down and under dramatically. I made it be pointed at the top, lessening to a fine line that reached to her navel. I looked around to make sure I was still where I was supposed to be, then settled my head back into the cradle of my left hand.

I began to phrase words carefully in my mind, projecting images somewhere behind my eyes to go with them.

"The surprising sensuality of her breasts was contrasted by her slimness."

"She had long arms and legs with long, flat muscles. But she was curvaceous at the same time."

I thought of the double curve of her upper arms, the long single curve of her forearms, and the recurve of her thumbs with their curved red nails.

That's it. Curves, an arrangement of curves, the curves and hollows of the body. I could see the powerfully feminine curves of Robin's calf muscles and suddenly understood the reason for the release of those opiumlike brain chemicals reported in magazines.

Her calves were set high on her legs, twin oblong curves of muscle, the insides slightly lower than the outsides, with a slight bulge to the inside matched by a more graceful curve to the outside offsetting the straight, slightly triangular plunge of her Achilles tendon down to her ankle.

Yes, I thought solemnly, that's it. Curves. The effect of curves on the brain.

I mentally compared Robin's long legs to the straight, shapeless shanks of Hawkins, who was revving up to speak, and felt a sense of joy.

Hawkins was no queen, but she would put me within one name of a bingo, and she was waving her arm in the air wildly. The name after hers on my card was a guy we didn't know well yet, but he was wearing a suit and had a briefcase under his chair. He looked like the type to get involved in the discussion.

I was positive it would be Hawkins when the professor looked down at his seating chart and called on Molly Severson. One row down and to the left Todd smiled and made an X on his card.

I was taken aback, not so much by the loss of Hawkins's X, but by Molly herself. She looked a lot like Robin, with the same lanky curviness, and was supposed to have been runner-up in the state beauty contest a few years back. She was beautiful, I thought, half-asleep, staring at her red spike heels. A lock of soft brown hair hung slightly out of place on her high white forehead.

But she was also grim and calculating, I remembered, an active member of the Women's Caucus that had warned Steve Galles against taping *Playboy* centerfolds up in his study carrel, and she once had the professor of this class, a man known as G. Bob, called on the carpet for making a joke in class.

It happened during a discussion of a legal provision binding the assignees in a real property problem. G. Bob rambled on about the situation for a while, then, removing his bifocals and assuming an attitude he intended as humorous, he asked how a tight skirt compared to the provision set forth in the property problem. Nobody responded as he paced back and forth a couple of times, so he beamed and said a tight skirt was similar because it bound the ass and knees.

Molly stood up before the words were all the way out of his mouth and told him his remarks were tasteless and discriminatory. Then she stomped out of the classroom and went directly upstairs to the dean's office.

G. Bob apologized to the entire class the next day, but it didn't seem to bother him much.

The point was, I thought, keeping a casual eye on my bingo card, that Molly's curves just didn't seem to have the same effect that Robin's did.

This necessitated a modification to my theory about attraction, and as G. Bob droned on about some rule of law he kept saying should be ignored, I tried to think of other things that drew me to Robin.

She made me laugh. That was important, definitely high on the list. And she was tough, like Molly, but more natural. Molly was artificial, the product of money, I thought indignantly. She was pretty tough when she was spouting some women's lib line, but she had straggled off like some wounded bird the night I asked her if she wanted to make a movie.

Well now, I thought, attraction is more than just curves. There are inner qualities to be considered. A simple-minded concept, I know. . . . The monologue rambled on in my head, blathering this way, then that. For a while I tried to set up an argument that I hadn't just plagiarized my ideas about desire from sleazy romance novels, that I had worked them out for myself. They were original. Then I thought, "Jesus Christ, they might be original, but they make me a master of the obvious," and on and on.

I came back to full consciousness when G. Bob, a bald man with a deceptive smile, called on a smallish, muscular red-headed guy named Jim who often played his guitar in the nooks around the law school. He seemed confused about whatever the question had been but kept trying to answer.

"No, I don't agree. I mean, that's about as bad as what happened to the Native Americans in this country," Jim said at one point.

The remark woke me up, and I raised my cheekbones out of the cup of my hands and put my chin there.

"I fail to see how the plight of the poor damned red man has anything to do with what I asked you," G. Bob snapped. A small but distinctive ball of spit had formed on his lower lip.

The remark seemed uncalled for, and people shifted uneasily throughout the room. Jim sat back ashen-faced and folded his arms across his chest.

Molly Severson lifted her head from a large brown casebook and looked at me from across the room.

Tyrone Patterson, president of the African American Caucus, swiveled in his seat and looked at me also, a pen clenched in his large white teeth.

Considering that I was the only Indian in the room, I guessed I had been informally chosen to say something. Mind racing, I moved around in my chair to reach the most upright position I could and considered a response.

I knew what Molly would do. She would stand up and fight back, go to the dean and complain. Tyrone and the other Black students were the ones who were really good at this, I thought. There were a lot of them and they were brave. They made things happen. But there were only five Indians in the entire school. I couldn't count on numbers.

Time passed with agonizing slowness as I tried frantically to think of something to base an argument on, something I could say that would set things straight on the issue of the poor damned red man.

All I could think of was seniority.

Seniority, I thought, damn, I can't argue that.

Then, in the brief moments as I struggled to mount an attack, Hawkins got the floor and broke in with a war story from her farm days.

As Hawkins began, Leonard Levine said "Bingo," in a subdued but clear voice. The other players began to crumple their cards among murmurs of displeasure.

"What, what's that?" G. Bob said.

"Did someone have something else to add?" He looked

around, confused, seemingly unaware of the bingo game, or of the animosity in front of him.

I folded my bingo card and stuck it in a notebook as I walked down the brown brick and tile hall after class. The colors were warm and earthy, but naked gray concrete beams overhead ruined the effect.

There were cobwebs on the walls and cigarette butts on the floor. The trash cans and shiny chrome cylindrical ashtrays were all overflowing. The place always seemed to need cleaning.

I thought to myself I would have been able to respond better during the discussion if the fucking place had offered the Native American law course they had promised. I had discovered during registration that the course listed in the law school catalog wasn't offered.

I talked to one of the deans about it, and he said, "Oh, yeah. We'll have to see if we can't do something about that." When the course wasn't offered again the next semester I went to see him again, but his secretary said he was busy. The course was never offered during the time I was in law school.

After a while I felt glad I hadn't gotten involved in the discussion. I didn't mind competition, and even a good dose of genuine dislike was nothing new. What I couldn't deal with was the spooky feeling that deep down most people actually believed that Indians were all dead, that they had died long ago, and that I was part of a vast nothingness.

Someone like me showing up was upsetting for everybody, I thought, including me. They had to examine me and I had to be examined; then came the dumb gratitude of accepting and being accepted, followed by the happiness of discovering there seemed to be no danger.

It was exhausting. I was supposed to be dead and I wasn't, or I wasn't supposed to be dead and I was but just hadn't realized it yet. In any case it was all wasted time, and after all the waste came the awful realization that I was not going to get one ounce of support from the law school beyond being allowed to be an affirmative action number.

That realization toward the end of the first year was debilitating. It was like the time when I was a kid and Leon died, I nearly died of a tonsillectomy, and Judy got sent away to the orphanage. It was like the time I got cut off the basketball team. I was screwed, I knew it, and there just wasn't much to be done but hang and rattle. I wanted to tear my teeth out. I wanted to run. I wanted to cry. I didn't know what I wanted to do. For lack of other options I decided I'd try to hang in there and graduate.

What was important at the moment, however, what had to be important, was that I had escaped into this hallway and it felt good to move away with the wisdom of silence. I hoped it would be hard for the others to tell if I was as smart as what I hadn't said.

The cynicism I demonstrated didn't develop overnight. At first, coming to law school seemed like a way of making something of myself. Now, hunched over a bar stool like Quasimodo, I wasn't so sure.

The morning's test had gone well, considering I had taken the course from a professor who, for personal reasons, often refused to grade examinations. The deans dealt with the need for grades by eventually issuing what they called an administrative pass, or sometimes by hiring someone else to do the grading.

Either option wasn't the best thing that could happen. An administrative pass was a kind of neutral two credits in a situation where grade point average meant everything—it didn't hurt but it didn't help, either. Having an outsider do the grading neutralized hard-earned information about how a professor graded. The worrying, like the situation, was feeble and really didn't lead anywhere.

G. Robert Harris was rare even among the power professors. Three or four of the teachers who were recognized authorities in their fields, had been at the law school for years, and were so firmly entrenched they did whatever they pleased in the classroom and got away with it.

A Calvinist red-neck nearing retirement age, G. Bob firmly believed he was one of the chosen. Given G. Bob's attitude and the subject matter he taught, to experience him in the classroom was like watching dinosaurs mate.

"This profession is like music," he stated on the first day of class. "Many purchase instruments but few will ever be able to play them properly. Ladies and gentlemen, look to the person on your left, then on your right, and be assured that only one of you will meet with success here."

We looked at each other and rolled our eyes, not knowing he had many invidious ways of fulfilling his prophecy. I had received low marks on one of the rare exams he did grade, and the next day went up to his office to talk to him about how I could have done better.

He was portly and bald, with rheumy eyes that bulged over bifocals pinched to the end of a bulbous nose. When he talked he stammered and spat aphorisms punctuated by a lengthy gutteral bass sound. His speech impediment was said to be the result of a deteriorating jaw bone.

"Good morning, Professor Harris," I said. "I'd like to talk to you about the examination?"

"Awww, well, I'm leaving for New York in a couple of hours, and I'd like to eat my lunch first," he replied.

"Well, it's kind of important," I said, trying to sound apologetic.

He looked genuinely exasperated and said, "Well, awww, if you insist, we'll have to look at it then, won't we?" He began to rummage through blue exam books piled in one corner of his office.

It took a long time to find my exam, and by the time G. Bob located it I knew I had made a mistake in approaching him. Finally he said, "Awww, yes, here it is."

There was nothing in the book that I could see, not even a grade number.

"Well, awww, as far as I can tell you didn't do much of anything right," he said after flipping the pages cursorily.

"What do you mean?" I said.

"Just what I said."

"What?" The room went slightly out of focus as anger washed over me.

"Awww, let me put it to you this way," he said. "Not everyone is cut out for this, you know. You look like a take-charge kinda guy. Maybe you oughta take charge of doing something else with your life."

"Oh," I said.

The happy-hour crowd was beginning to fill Bullwinkle's, and two students I knew slightly walked in and nodded a greeting. I was tight and greeted them generously. The tall thin one was a Notre Dame graduate, supposedly some kind of genius.

"Very nice to see you gentlemen this evening," I said, enjoying the sound of my own voice. My mouth was sour, and I reached for one of the menthol cigarettes I had purchased from the machine. One of them said something in a foreign language that seemed to have something to do with smoking, and they moved on.

As I turned back to the bar I noticed a solitary figure standing by one of the booths near the door. It was Preston, one of the other Indian students at the law school. There were five of us, and we were named Larson, Johnson, Anderson, Anderson, and DuFour. Preston was the DuFour, and I walked over to him to ask if he wanted a beer.

"How about a beer," I said, happy to have the company.

Preston looked around nervously, and I thought for a moment he wanted to be left alone. Then he said in a strange tone of voice, "It seems as if . . ." and his voice trailed off to nothing.

"Lemme get you one," I repeated. "Whatcha drinking?"

He kind of gathered himself then and looked directly at me. "It seems as though I'm having a problem."

"How's that, Preston?" I responded.

He looked away again, and I edged the short distance to a place at the bar. I was thinking we all had problems, and I hoped Preston wasn't going to insist on dwelling on them tonight.

I got a couple of beers and made my way back through the

crowd. "So what's going on, pard?" I said, trying to think of a way to change Preston's mood.

He looked at me weirdly and said, "It seems as though I went to the doctor yesterday, but it didn't help."

"Oh," I said, struggling to understand what was going on. "Something the matter?"

"Apparently I can't get my canned memo done," he said, "although I really don't know why."

The canned memo was a writing assignment we were all currently struggling with, and it was kind of frustrating trying to figure out what you were supposed to do with it. But everybody was complaining about that. What struck me funny was the way Preston was talking, like his words were being filtered through something.

"Hey Preston, you feeling okay?" I said obtusely.

"It seems as though I'm paranoid schizophrenic," he said flatly.

"Hey, come on. Who told you that shit?" I asked.

"It seems as if I went to the doctor a few days ago but it didn't help . . ." His voice trailed off again.

"Let's go over here and sit down," I said.

He kept repeating the same fragments over and over again in a small choking voice. Some other guys I knew came in and sat down with us. After listening to Preston talk for a while one of them said he thought we should get him to a doctor.

"Aw, man," I said. "I don't know."

But it got worse. Preston said he wanted to go for a walk and left Bullwinkle's. It seemed like a good idea and nobody paid any attention until a third-year student came in and said there was some Indian raising hell over in the law library.

A couple of us got up and began to get ready to go see what was going on, but about that time Preston came back into Bullwinkle's. The guy that had told us about the problem said, "That's him. He was cussing and throwing books around. I think they called security."

I waved Preston over to the booth and he slumped in the corner, holding himself with both arms. I tried to talk to him, but he just sat there repeating his broken phrases. Somebody suggested we take him to the hospital again and I said, "No, goddammit. Just leave him alone."

About that time Preston took two or three bottles of pills out of his pockets and began to fool around with them.

"Jesus," somebody said, picking up one of the bottles. "This is some serious shit."

"I'm going to take all of them," Preston said. "Every last one."

We took him to Hennepin County General Hospital then, and after about an hour a doctor came to the psychiatric waiting room and said, "Gentlemen, your friend is crazier than hell."

We drove back to Bullwinkle's and sat in the same corner spot, smoking and saying very little. Outside a neon hot dog flashed yellow and red, and I ordered whiskey.

Ghost Dancer

It was late when I woke up. The motel room was hot and smelled like stale cigar smoke. In the corner some guy on television kept clutching his head and telling himself what he thought he was hearing the audience say about men wearing women's clothing.

I staggered into the bathroom and turned on the cold water. The plastic glasses kept breaking when I tried to get the sanitary covering off, so I filled the sink with water and drank. My dripping face and bloodshot eyes looked like hell in the mirror. I turned to the toilet bowl and threw up the water.

I pulled back the heavy dark curtain that kept the room semi-dark to try and see where I was. A sign said "Gopher Motel," but I didn't recognize the street names. I circled the room a couple of times, confused, then sat back down on the bed and held my head in my hands. I couldn't keep a train of thought going for more than a few seconds at a time, except for the pervasive feeling that something was wrong.

I felt like I was suffocating, so I turned the cold water on in the shower and stepped underneath. As I aimed the cool spray at the top of my head I remembered the girl, well-groomed, curvy, telling me to talk to her as she clutched and swooped beneath me.

She had come into Bullwinkle's with a slick-looking character who said he was from Panama or someplace like that. She told him what a lousy time she had in Acapulco because he wouldn't speak English, and he flew into a rage and stormed out, leaving the two of us alone. It was like wet silk between her legs.

Preston had awakened a whirl of old feelings—a gelatinous paranoid mass of anger, pain, and fear that I had learned long ago was better left alone. Seeing Preston the way he was scared me, and I had medicated myself into oblivion with alcohol.

I thought about self-control and remembered an article I had been reading that said it was easy. At a clinic in California people learned how to control smoking, weight, blood pressure, headaches, asthma, chronic pain, alcohol and drug dependency, sleep disturbances, bed-wetting, muscle tics, depression, anxiety, anger, phobias, dieting, sexual problems, and more.

It took about three seconds, they said, after a thought arises in the brain, to identify the thought, decide to change it, and make the change. They had observed the process in clients attached to scientific equipment that registered changes with audible tones and jumping meters. The client can reverse thoughts most simply, they said. Instead of thinking "this is terrible," she could think, "this is exciting." Even if it wasn't.

This was all supposed to have worked on some Indian named Sari who now was able to produce strong erections and had mastered full information about how to stimulate his bride-to-be. I turned my face up to the spray of water, swallowed hard, and decided not to puke. I gave it the required three seconds, then slipped down to one knee and heaved in great wrenching spasms.

The intramural football season was slated to begin at 4:30 P.M. I glanced at my watch. It was now nearly 2:30. I had arrived in court six hours earlier to prosecute a simple-minded speeding case and it had gotten out of hand.

The defendant had been pulled over for speeding in the vicinity of an electric generating plant, and he claimed that all that electricity could have caused the radar gun to go haywire.

He had also turned out to be a litigator for one of the largest law firms in the Twin Cities. He had a young associate from his firm with him as his counsel, and she and I were getting an educational experience.

"Objection, your honor," I asserted loudly. "Although officer Sterud is a well-trained radar operator, he is not an electrical engineer."

The attorney for the defendant, a tall blonde woman, didn't even slow down, and kept introducing charts and figures that obviously no one in the courtroom understood, including her.

"Counsel, you will not object while the defense is still talking," the judge said to me. "The objection is overruled. Officer, you may answer if you can."

I looked over my shoulder at Sandra Hutton. She was pissed off because she had to cancel her afternoon calendar to do student attorney duty with me through this thing. I checked her out and wondered when it was I had lost my charm.

My witness, a thin, middle-aged cop from St. Paul, had been cross-examined way beyond anything he was used to, and he was beginning to crumble. These guys related the facts of an arrest and then watched the defendant take his lumps a hundred times a month, and any deviation from that routine only added to their cynicism.

As opposing counsel finished her interrogation, she turned and looked at me from a height. I shuffled some notes from one pile into another and tried to look like I knew what I was going to do next.

"Does the defense wish to rest?" the judge asked flatly.

"No, your honor," replied the big blonde girl, "but what we would like to do, in consideration of the fact we feel very strongly the prosecution has not satisfied the elements of the charge, is to ask your honor for a directed verdict of not guilty at this time."

"I ahh, but I . . . ," I stammered as the judge cut me off in mid-sentence.

"Counsel, your motion for a verdict of not guilty is granted, the charges are dropped, and the defendant is free to go." The judge rose quickly and swirled into her chambers, slamming the door behind her. All the air in the room seemed to whirl out with her.

I turned and looked at Sandra. She was grimacing openly now.

"I told you she would find this way, didn't I?" She spoke to her legal pad as she headed for the judge's chambers. "Wait in my office."

The defendant, a dapper-looking guy with an air of confidence, strode up to me and extended his hand. I shook it and tried to pull back my cracked lips.

"You did a good job," he said out of one side of his tanned face while grinning at his assistant out of the other. "You got your ass kicked but you picked up some pointers, didn't you?"

"I'll say," I said, wondering how he would like my briefcase upside his head.

"Don't worry," he said. "I started right here myself fifteen years ago."

"That's encouraging," I said.

We finished gathering up our things and moved to the door at the rear of the courtroom.

"Bye," the big girl smiled as she closed the door on me. I paused for a moment and looked around, thinking that if this was what practicing law was all about, it wasn't a fun way to spend your life.

I took the elevator to Sandra's office and stood there looking at the rooftop of the building below. The lines and shapes were unnatural and did not seem to fit in with the other buildings that were visible, or with the gray sky above, or with anything else.

Sandra entered the room with her clipped, high-heeled stride, and I moved back and took a chair as much off to one side of the small room as I could get.

"Judge Hayes told me she felt we just didn't overcome the minimum possibility of distortion to the radar device language in the statute," she said, leaning on a coat tree as she changed her heels for red and white running shoes.

This was my cue to get interested in the elements of the case, but instead I looked at her slightly curved legs with the feet that pointed sideways when she walked. Her breasts seemed to have the same tendency as she reached up to hang her coat.

"Did you have any questions for me?" she asked, turning to find me staring at her.

"Ah, well, ah, I guess I was a little surprised," I said. "But it was a good experience," I quickly added.

She smiled then, and rocked her swivel chair back, fixing an analytical gaze on me as her hands nestled in her lap. She looked kind of goofy sitting there in her power clothing with her feet sticking out sideways in colorful running shoes that did not quite touch the floor.

"Well," I said. "I know you have things to do, and I have a touch football game in a couple of hours."

"Oh," she smiled. "Are you a football player?"

"Well, kind of, I guess. Used to be anyway."

"Football seems kind of stupid to me."

"Ah, well, ya, I guess it is."

I swiveled my head and looked out the window again. I imagined myself running across the tarred expanse, vaulting the mouthlike ducts, leaping from building to building.

Suddenly, there seemed to be very little reason to be sitting in a stuffy office smothering in a cheap Malaysian suit, or studying law, or for having come to this uptight place to start with.

Running across rooftops seemed to be the thing to do, even as I mouthed my thanks to Sandra for all her help. I could see her lips moving, but I didn't listen to her anymore as I removed my overcoat from the rack and walked out, smiling, mentally leaping from roof to roof.

During the drive back to campus, I felt more upbeat than I had for quite a while, but that wasn't saying much. I didn't care about the case. It seemed about right that some high-powered character had gotten off because he had the resources to come into court and defend a twenty-dollar ticket all day long.

I had got what I came for. Sandra told me her evaluation of my performance would be good. "That's what I have learned so far," I thought. "Take care of number one." There was a saying around school that the first year they tried to scare you to death, the second year they tried to work you to death, and the third year they tried to bore you to death. The last part seemed to be true. It wasn't what I had expected.

Parking wasn't easy in a place where there were sixty thousand students and maybe ten thousand parking spots. Driving wasn't easy either. As I backed into an opening I remembered the first words someone spoke to me when I got here. They had come from a group of blacks in a white Lincoln, who had shouted at me, "Learn how to drive, motherfucker!"

I began shedding the suit as I walked toward the building. The Midwest summer heat was like a moist embrace in the late afternoon. Inside it was too cool. A group of first-year students were gathered in the floating lounge, talking, laughing, and measuring each other carefully.

Downstairs another group of defeated-looking second-year students bitched quietly to themselves on the wooden mushrooms in front of the bookstore. I got my sweatclothes from my locker and went into the bathroom to change.

I hung the damp suit in my locker and went to the intramural board to check the schedule. We weren't playing for an hour yet, so there was time to go to Bullwinkle's for the pre-game. The nucleus of the team would be there and so would Robin, barmaid with the body of a gymnast.

Outside, the air was still heavy, but I felt loose and free in my gear as I jogged and dodged through the Corners area to Bullwinkle's. I stepped inside and pushed my Minnesota Twins cap back against the gloom. The place was full, and I had to squeeze sideways into a place at the beat-up wooden bar.

"Jackie, you're the best bartender I've ever seen," I called.

Jackie turned from the far end of the bar and smiled her great smile. Her brown ponytail flipped under her chin and back again.

"Hey, whatcha gonna have?" she said.

"I want you and I want you now."

"Uh oh, the Moose is loose again," she said to Robin, who was unloading a tray full of empty glasses into the waitress station next to me.

"Well, hi there," I said to Robin, thinking this was working out just right.

Robin looked at me like I had two heads and turned back to Jackie with a bored look on her face.

"Jackie, I'll have one of those diet beers, and get Robin here a shot of Rebel Yell."

"I'm not allowed to drink on duty," Robin said, and turned her back on me.

122

I winced in Jackie's direction, and she laughed and handed me my beer and a glass.

"Charge this to the Inflatable Dragons, will you? It's part of my contract."

"Sure," she said, turning to write on a note pad next to the cash register. The Dragons always had a tab on game nights.

I climbed the steps to the Moose's nest in search of the Dragons. They sat in back of the neon coney dog that illuminated Bullwinkle's front window. It was believed that the neon rays helped preparation for important events and also cured hangovers. Whipper Scharue was there, Wiener Wiewick, big Todd Piper, and some unfamiliar faces, which I was glad to see. The touch football league was vicious, and replacements were important.

A recruit was asking Todd something about sports as I sat down.

"So you're from Glendale, huh?"

"Yup," replied Todd.

"Who was the big guy, their all-stater four or five years ago when they beat Hutchinson for the championship?"

"Me," Todd said, rising from his chair. "Inflate, Dragons."

"Oh." The reply was lost in the scuffling of chairs.

We filed out into the muggy evening and made our way toward the playing field across from the law school. Neon was jumping bright from all the angles of Seven Corners, dominated by a red cowboy roping a steer over the display windows of an appliance store. The place used to be called Snoose Boulevard and was like the hub of a wheel with six bars surrounding a circular intersection.

"Didn't Glendale have a super baseball pitcher about that

time, too?" The new guy had caught up with Todd again. "Didn't he throw a pitch so hard he broke his collar bone and ruined his career?"

"Yup."

"Who was that guy, anyway?"

"Me," Todd said, turning to Whipper Scharue. "Hey Whip, who's got the beer?" he asked.

"You guys always drink like this?" The new guy was about a foot and a half shorter than Todd.

"I gotta believe it makes this bunch play better," Todd said, staring straight ahead.

The intramural fields were part grass and part sand. Todd rounded up the new guys and was throwing footballs at them to see who could catch. Most of them seemed surprised when the ball blasted through their hands and glanced off their chests, the beginnings of a blue bruise spreading on their breastbones.

They didn't know it yet, but if they dropped the first ball they would be linemen as long as they played for the Dragons. Todd ran a tight ship on the football field, verging on cruel. We blamed the high turnover of players on our team on him.

We were ahead near the end of the first half when two gridders began to converse intently off by themselves. They were going at it pretty good, but their hands were firmly set on their hips. When the hands came up was when trouble usually began.

"Oh yeah, how'd you like me to knock your dick in the dirt!" screamed Eric, an ex-hockey player with Daniel Webster eyebrows. He was one of ours.

"I'll tear your head off and take a shit in it," Eric's redheaded opponent yelled back. They both had extremely bowed legs.

Todd took advantage of the argument to jog over and grab my beer.

"Don't you think you oughta play a little more, fat boy?" he said.

"I think I might be injured," I said.

"Come on, I'll throw you a few."

The two guys who had been arguing were shaking hands as I made my way onto the field, but a third guy was holding his nose and being attended to by the referee. "Who would be dumb enough to get between those two," I thought. A first-year player frowned as he saw me heading for his position, and he automatically left for the sideline.

"Let's try and go deep for another score," Todd said in the huddle, looking at me. "Doakie and Whip cross behind."

"Don't forget me out there, okay?" I said.

"You got it," he said, smiling. He liked to send me deep every play to open up his short game.

As soon as I split wide, one of their defensive backs ran up to change places with the linebacker in front of me. I had burned these guys earlier, and they were all yelling and pointing in my direction.

I saw the snap and sprinted out. I was looking off to the sideline like I might go there, thinking I might fake this guy out, when both of them ran over me. The floodlights were very brilliant overhead for a moment, then shattered as I landed on the grass.

I got to my hands and knees and waited for my vision to return, then staggered upright in time to see Todd throw his favorite short pass. "Whyn't you watch where you're going," he instructed as I wobbled for the sideline.

I went to the beer cooler and sat down. The grass sidehill felt good as I rubbed my jaw and thought about how I seemed to be getting blindsided a lot lately.

"Postgame at Bullwinkle's," Todd said to the players when the game was over. The new guy was at his elbow, starting to ask questions again. We had lost by two touchdowns.

The Dragons walked back toward the bar, an odd combination of sizes, shapes, and colors. Almost everyone had a piece of uniform from some team or other they had played on in the past, but nobody wore the same thing. It was strictly every man for himself.

The nine o'clock lull was on at Bullwinkle's as we filed inside and mounted the stairs to the nest. We milled around at the top, waiting for organization.

"Uh, you folks will have to leave now," Todd said to a small group occupying the cramped space behind the neon sign. The people looked around nervously and sat tight.

I moved to the rail and looked down on the bar below. At the far end opposite the door Jackie and Robin were sitting with a couple of large frothy drinks apiece in front of them.

"Todd," I said intently.

"Boys, defend the nest," Todd said as he spotted the girls. "We've got some business to attend to."

We walked the length of the bar on the upper deck and descended the steep back stairs three at a time.

"Allow us to buy you a drink, ladies," I said.

126

"Have I ever told you how much I admire women who work?" Todd said to Jackie, putting his arms around both girls.

They looked at each other, smiled and scooted their stools together to make room for us. My cleats clacked on the worn tile floor as I moved next to Robin and waved to the bartender.

Over my shoulder I heard Todd say, "Jackie, let me ask you this." The rest of his words were lost as Robin looked up at me and smiled. I put one arm around her waist and signaled the bartender for another round with the other.

Taped music swelled with the crowd as we talked intently, the liquor a flame racing ahead of old high school stories, a running commentary about what assholes bar customers were, and scattered bits of philosophy. My hands returned again and again to the muscular ridges on either side of Robin's backbone. I caressed her bare arms to emphasize my wild stories. I was happy.

I finally looked up and realized Todd and Jackie were gone. I hadn't stopped smiling for at least an hour, and my face was starting to hurt. I caught a glimpse of us in the back bar mirror.

Two wings of longish hair stuck out over my ears from beneath the blue Twins cap. Robin's face appeared to be slightly lopsided in the reflection as she chattered between puffs of a cigarette.

"I wasn't supposed to live when I was born," she said, digging into her purse. "Oh, damn!" she exclaimed, as she lost her grip and spilled the contents onto the floor.

I dropped to one knee and began gathering up her wallet and change as she stood unsteadily. I looked up directly onto the swell of her tanned thighs as she put her hand on my shoulder to regain

127

her balance. A pattern of blonde hairs swirled down her legs. I stood up and handed her the purse.

"Let's get out of here. I've got some beers in the cooler in my car."

"Good idea," she said. "I think I could use some air."

My old four-door Mercury was parked behind Bullwinkle's. I tried not to step on Robin as we walked unsteadily down the sidewalk. I put my arm around her shoulders and she hooked her left thumb in one of my belt loops.

"This is the Mercury Hotel," I said when we got to the car. "And, oh, the tales it could tell if it could only talk!"

She laughed and we slid in and got ready to take off. The car had electric everything, and we turned it all on as we left Bullwinkle's. Wipers, music, windows opening and closing, seat going up and down.

I drove to Stillwater and we crossed the St. Croix to the Wisconsin side. There was a place to park on the bluff above the river that looked down on the lights of the waterfront below.

We found KOMA, Oklahoma City, on the radio, and I slid us over to the passenger side. A big hoop earring hung from Robin's left ear, and it caught the moonlight whenever she turned her head.

I pointed to the moon and started to tell her about her earring when she looked at me kind of funny and said, "I think I'm going to be sick."

"Oh shit," I thought.

"Want me to open the door?"

She nodded urgently and covered her mouth with both hands.

I grabbed the handle and shoved the heavy door open as she fell halfway out, wretching violently.

I didn't know what to do, so I caressed her great ass while she heaved. After a while she sputtered a couple of times and sat up in the seat shivering.

I handed her a stiff towel from a pile of gym stuff in the back and she wiped her face and blew her nose.

"It's okay," I said. "Just relax and we'll get you home."

"No," she said, turning and pressing herself against me.

"I want you to love me," she slurred, sliding her hands up under my shirt. "I want you to love me now," she said, offering me her mouth.

I avoided the kiss and reached into the glovebox. There was an old pack of Rolaids among papers, some coins, and a stale pack of cigarettes.

"Here," I said, handing her a Rolaid. "Eat this, it'll make you feel better."

I put one in her mouth and she began to chew.

"Have another one. These things are really good for an upset stomach."

She had curled up next to me and was already asleep by the time I offered her the second Rolaid. I listened to KOMA for a while, smoked a cigarette, and started for town.

The moon was very bright on the way back to Minneapolis. I couldn't help feeling I had lost my rhythm somewhere among all these lakes. I was up to my old tricks again, and I knew that wasn't good. I drove very carefully, my unconscious prize sleeping peacefully next to me.

Catch Colt

There was a note on the message board in the downstairs hall. The board was about five feet by ten feet, polished oak like all the other wood in the building, and on its little metal hooks was posted information that could make you or break you.

Overhead, the imposing brick and glass law building spilled downhill to the south. It was terraced in an arrangement of cubicles that looked like a cliff dwelling.

The note with my name on it in the L column said to report to Helen Fuller's office to discuss my application for employment with the Department of Natural Resources. Helen had arranged the application. She spoke with a lisp, and I thought she was attractive.

The administrative offices were never as neat as I thought they should be, and the fact nagged at me as I walked toward the rear for my appointment. "People like this could easily lose my loan applications," I thought, "and I would be sunk."

I caught the eye of the secretary as I moved through. She was connected by headphones to a large black machine that clicked and plunged beneath her hands. Her mastery of the machine made her strong, and she stared me down easily.

"Hello there," Helen said. "Please sit down."

She was very feminine, with a slight overbite that seemed to go with her personality.

"Hi," I said, averting my eyes and trying to pull my smile past the antagonistic grin I had seen reflected in a mirror once.

"Let me see, there was something I wanted to talk to you about," she said, shuffling through a file folder that had my name written on it in flowing longhand.

"Oh, yes, here it is. Were you interested in getting on the list to interview for this position?"

"Yeah, I guess so," I mumbled.

"Well, if you are, there are some things that might be helpful to you," she said, looking at me intently.

I could tell she was trying to figure out what was going on with me. I wondered if she could tell I was convinced there was no danger of getting this job and that I didn't much care anyway.

There had been a position I was interested in and I jumped through all the hoops to try and make a good impression. The initial stuff seemed to go real well, and I was surprised when my contact person called and said they had eliminated me from the short list.

We had hit it off during interviews, and she agreed to talk to me when I asked her if she would meet me after work to discuss what had happened. It was simple, she said. When they asked the law school for a reference, the official word was, "Sid really didn't get involved like we hoped he would."

No shit. What did that mean? I didn't get credit for graduating?

"That's all they had to say," she said. "And competition for this position being what it is, that's all we needed to hear."

I listened to Helen for a while longer and left. I had some vague guilt, a feeling that seemed to be growing as I moved away from the building and prepared to settle in at Bullwinkle's.

But it was spring, graduation was only a couple weeks away, and I didn't have much to do until then except figure out what I was going to do with my life next. I fingered the few dollars in my

Levi's pocket. They would get me by if I utilized the afternoon beer specials carefully. The bar was wooden dark and smoky as I entered. The women were not very beautiful.

I sat next to a nervous man wearing aviator glasses and a dark purple leather coat. The man's voice made him seem larger than he really was. His coat smelled strongly of some type of chemical, and he kept telling me it was best to call a spade a shovel. I agreed and the man called for a round of drinks.

"Leinenkugel for me, Jackie," I said. They were two for one.

"Well *shitfire,* I just don't know," the man with the leather coat yelled. "Tell you what, just pour a couple of shots of Blackberry Brandy in a glass, would you sweetheart? I been feelin' a little under the weather all day."

"No wonder," I thought.

He had said his name was Gene Lyle, and I watched him drink about eight shots of some kind of brandy that was almost the same color as his coat. He was eating Rolaids at the same time and telling about his son, whom he referred to as meathead.

"Meathead's a good kid," he said, "works for Cyclone Fence."

"Cyclone Fence?"

"Sure, those chain-link jobs. You know. Makes six bucks an hour with a raise in July."

"Oh, I see," I replied.

"Meathead's a good kid, but Jeanita, that's the daughter, now she's a different story."

"Oh," I said.

"Oh God, yes," he repeated. "When you get to be my age, pal, you'll get your turn. I'll tell you what. I wouldn't take a million dollars for the kids I got, but I wouldn't give ten cents for another one."

He threw back his head and guffawed loudly, and it made me laugh. "I s'pose so," I said.

Gene Lyle ordered another round of drinks and told me of his rise from Electrolux vacuum cleaner salesman to farm and ranch realtor, and about his brother Faron who had been shot to death in the Alibi Club in St. Paul.

Suddenly, a square of brilliant light appeared at the end of the bar and in walked a middle-aged woman with peroxide blonde hair.

"Honey!" Gene bawled. "Come over here and meet my friend. What's your name again, pal?" he slurred, looking at me intently.

The woman was Gene's wife, and she didn't look too happy as she sat down and lit a cigarette. Gene started to tell about the details of the blast that had killed his brother. He told the story well, dabbing at his eyes with a Budweiser napkin, but the beer was beginning to affect me and I became lost in my own stare from the back bar mirror.

Gene's story reminded me of my grandmother telling about Ed Shambo getting shot out at the Hays Post Office. I could hear her in my mind like she was sitting next to me.

"I sent your mother to Seattle to Curt and Mary's to have you. I thought it best. When you got back I made her give you your father's name. I paid for having it done."

I couldn't help but think of my father then, and how I had never heard from him or laid eyes on him until I tracked him down a few months ago. I thought about how Gros Ventres call illegitimate children "Catch Colt," and thought that's what I was, someone caught on the edge of a marginal people.

He had been an enigmatic figure in the few stories I had been told about him, a mystery, a question, a potential source of answers, and unfinished business related to my childhood. I had thought about him a lot, first from one angle of vision, then another, but always cautiously, in the manner of one planning risky business.

When I was in high school one of my aunts gave me two photographs of my father and my mother. One had been taken in front of the Bluebird Cafe in Dodson, Montana, she explained. In the other, they were posed in front of an artificial backdrop of a fair scene complete with a ferris wheel and roller coaster.

The faces in the pictures looked very young, and I thought I could see myself in my father's high forehead and dimpled grin. My mother and this particular aunt were often at odds, and I remember being suspicious of her motivation in giving me the photographs, although I was ecstatic to have them under any circumstances.

After my grandmother died and I had dropped out of college, one of the first things I did was look up my paternal grandfather, who I had heard lived in Kalispell, Montana. I found the old man's name in the telephone book, and he invited me to his apartment, where we visited for a while.

He told me where his youngest son lived. Then he asked me if I had gone to school with him. I replied that I had not, but that I thought he was my father. He said he didn't know Buddy had gotten anyone in trouble, but he agreed to tell him he had spoken to me when he saw him next.

After I moved to Brookings, which was tantalizingly close to where my father lived, I wrote him a letter asking to meet him but received no response. Time passed and I moved on to law school in Minneapolis, still more or less postponing a confrontation. But, my Master's thesis adviser at South Dakota, who had become aware of my father through my writing, encouraged me to look him up, and finally I decided to do it.

On the pretext of attending homecoming activities at South Dakota State, I left Minneapolis one afternoon without telling anyone what I was really up to and drove to Fergus Falls, Minnesota. I stopped at a grain elevator on the outskirts of town, got directions to Bud Larson's farm, and drove there straightaway.

It was dark when I drove into the farmyard. I left my car running, knocked at the door, and was greeted by a middle-aged woman. I asked if Bud was there, she said yes, and he walked into the kitchen, removing his reading glasses as he entered.

I told him my name was Sid Larson and watched carefully for a response. He showed none. I asked him if he remembered a gal named Toodles, or Buck or Sis Cole from Montana. He hesitated and cocked his head quizzically.

At that point, glancing from him to his wife, I asked him if he would mind stepping outside with me, that there was something I wanted to talk to him about. He stepped into the other room to put on a pair of leather moccasins, and we walked outside. A sidewalk maybe twenty yards long led to my car. About halfway to the end of the sidewalk I told him I thought he was my father.

He looked up at me and said nothing. He leaned back against my car, facing his house, while I had my back to it. I explained that all I wanted was to meet him, that I felt I had "unfinished business" with him. He replied that he could understand my point of view and said I "looked like something to be proud of."

I made small talk based on the information I had been given by his father and my family. He replied, "So, you got the story on me, huh?"

I said there wasn't much, but yes, I guessed so.

"What am I supposed to tell my wife?"

I told him I was thirty-two years old and that probably whatever had happened was before her time but that he was welcome to tell her I was a relative or whatever he wanted, that I didn't want to cause him any trouble.

I told him that I was in the phone book in Minneapolis and would like to hear from him. He replied that he was a country boy and never got to the Twin Cities. I shook his hand and told him I appreciated his good nature.

As I turned to get in my car, which was still running, I could see his wife had cranked open a side window of the house and was sitting there observing. Our eyes met briefly and I walked away.

A sharp clap on the back jarred me out of the trance I had fallen into, and I turned quickly to find Gene Lyle mumbling at me through chalk-flecked lips.

"I'm bombed," he said wearily. "Time to head 'em up and move 'em out."

"Drive careful," I said, watching him hit all four walls on the way out.

Sweat Lodge

Although I still thought law school had done me wrong, there wasn't much to be done about it. I wanted more, of course, and tended to take personally what I saw as lack of a payoff, while to the institution, I think, it was business as usual. It seemed as though they thought I should be grateful for simply having been allowed to attend.

After a while, I was. I came to have the feeling that Gene Lyle expressed in Bullwinkle's one afternoon—I wouldn't take a million dollars for my legal education, but I wouldn't pay a dime for another one. Be that as it may, I graduated from law school in the spring of 1985, and, faced with a nonexistent market for

Indian lawyers in Minneapolis, returned to Brookings, South Dakota.

It was a time when banks in the Midwest were busy repossessing farms against which they had convinced farmers to borrow outrageous sums of money. When the market changed and the loans could not be repaid, those banks took none of the responsibility, pursuing their legal option of foreclosure instead.

A friend of mine, David Leggett, represented one of these banks, which was finding it necessary to defend lender liability suits brought by farmers trying to save themselves from foreclosure. He had a thriving individual bankruptcy practice as well, and, in response to a growing case load, he hired me to help with the work.

Leggett was a good attorney and a good man, a genuinely caring person who probably should never have gone into the practice of law in the first place. He told me once he had seriously considered the priesthood, and I think that may have been his true calling. Or, it could have been that his appetite for Canadian Club whiskey would have overhauled him eventually in any circumstance. At any rate, I liked him, and we worked well together.

In fact, within a period of a couple of years, we acquired the downtown property where the law office was located, a steak house, and an option on other property for a fast-food business. Given the way things were going, it was kind of strange when Leggett stopped coming to work.

He wasn't above taking a trip somewhere or otherwise disappearing when his calendar was light, so nobody thought much about it until the days stretched into a week, then two weeks, then three. By then it was clear something was amiss, and finally his parents approached me about what should be done.

Having spent some time around alcoholics, it didn't seem impossible to me that Leggett was holed up somewhere on a drunk, so I started making phone calls around the area. A few days later a guy I had tended bar with called and said he had seen Dave in Watertown, about sixty miles north of Brookings.

The family decided the alcoholics anonymous strategy of an "intervention team" was the way to handle things, and they asked me to be part of the team. I wasn't so sure Leggett shouldn't just be left alone to work things out for himself, but the pressure was mounting from clients, the bank, and his parents, so I agreed to do it.

It turned out that me being part of the team meant I would spearhead the intervention while the others waited outside. I had located Leggett in the Holiday Inn in Watertown, and on the appointed day we all drove up there and they sent me to the door. I knocked and said, "David, it's me. Open up."

He opened the door and greeted me warmly. There were two half-gallons of Canadian Club and three or four liters of 7-Up lined up neatly on the writing table next to the television. "Mr. Ed," his favorite television program, was on and he shushed me as we walked into the room. I almost told him to run for it.

He added more liquor to his glass and poured me one as he waved me to a chair next to the bed. I sat there stupidly, sipping my drink, as the rest of the alcohol intervention team waited outside for my signal. Leggett was adamant about not being interrupted during "Mr. Ed," and I must have sat there for fifteen minutes waiting for the program to end.

Finally, it was over and I said, "Pardner, there's something I have to tell you and I don't think you're going to like it much. Your folks and your sisters are outside with an alcohol counselor." His face fell and he looked away.

After a while he said, "Well, I suppose you better go get 'em."

I went out to the parking lot and led the group back to the room. Leggett was staring at the television with his hands clasped behind his head. He didn't say anything.

His father began to speak, mumbling a few ineffectual words, then demanded that the counselor take over and explain what was going on. A long parlay followed, apparently following a scenario that had been rehearsed at the counselor's office.

I felt out of place and thought the whole thing was kind of stupid until Leggett began to seem to accept what was going on. At that point he opened the drawer to the bedside table, took out a .38 pistol and his microcassette recorder, and handed them to me. "Go ahead and play the tape," he said. "You might as well know what I was going to do."

The recorder contained a suicide tape that explained in detail how unhappy Leggett was. He talked about how all he had done was work, then work and drink, until he felt it was too late to do anything else. He was convinced he would never have a family because of it, said how he hated what he was doing, then said he just wanted out. He was thirty-six years old.

I was stunned, and everybody else in the room looked like they were too. The counselor kept talking, and he eventually got Leggett to agree to ride to the treatment center in Sioux Falls with him. I drove back to Brookings alone, the gun and recorder on the seat beside me, trying to figure out what in the world would cause Leggett to want to do himself in.

As I thought about it, I thought of the last case we had handled for the bank. It was the latest in a series of foreclosures where the bank took everything from farmers who were not able to pay mortgages. The farmer's name was Marvin Gunderson, and he was big and raw-boned, probably sixty years old. He was a simple man, a hard worker who had farmed in the area for more than forty years. When the bank was finished with him, he had a ten-year-old Ford car and an apartment in subsidized housing paid for by welfare.

We never lost a single one of these cases, but by the time we finished the Gunderson trial, I think Leggett and I had both about had it with that kind of victory. It was awful watching the old farmer try to fight such an uneven battle, and if there had been a way to tell opposing counsel how to win, and I knew a way that might have worked, I think I might actually have considered doing so.

After Leggett checked into the treatment center things really got crazy. I suddenly had both our workloads, his family decided I was at least partially to blame for his drinking, accounts receivable fell off by about 30 percent, and our creditors began circling like sharks.

In the midst of this I got a telephone call from the treatment center a couple of weeks after Leggett checked in. The caller was the assistant supervisor of the center. She asked me if I was Mr. Larson, then said, "I called to ask you if you could drive down and pick up Mr. Leggett."

"What did you say?" I replied.

"Could you come and get Mr. Leggett."

"What for?" I asked cautiously.

"I'm afraid we just can't have Mr. Leggett in the program, and we have asked him to leave."

"What do you mean?" I said, alarmed at her tone.

"Mr. Leggett is completely unmanageable, and I'm afraid he has become a negative influence on other clients."

"Yes," I said carefully, trying to think what to do, "but isn't that what you people do? I mean, aren't you in business to handle this kind of thing?" I knew what had happened. Leggett was slick, and it was Randle P. McMurphy in the *Cuckoo's Nest* all over again.

"Oh no," she said. "I'm afraid you may have misunderstood what we do here."

"The hell you say," I replied. "What about the five grand we paid you?"

"Well, I'm afraid that money is nonrefundable, you see. It was . . ."

"Bullshit!" I yelled, practically hysterical. "I'll sue you and your chicken-shit treatment center into the next century!"

After I lost it, the woman transferred me to the director of the center. I blustered and threatened again, and finally the guy agreed to transfer Leggett to the center's facility in Rapid City, on the other side of the state.

Two days later a man from the bank called and made an appointment to see me. He was an assistant vice president, and he walked into my office about one o'clock that afternoon. He wanted to talk about Leggett, asking me what was going on and what I thought would happen. I explained I thought things would work out given a little time.

The bank officer seemed genuinely concerned about Leggett, and I explained that I thought having to face his problem was probably the best thing that could have happened. He agreed. We talked about other business matters, and then he began to make leaving noises. As he stood up, he said, "By the way, David's notes are ninety days overdue, and if we don't receive payment by Friday we'll have to start foreclosure on the house and car. I'm sure you understand."

I looked at him without saying anything. He turned then and left, and I thought, boy, that's gratitude for you. I thought for a few minutes more, then called Leggett's dad. His father was worth over a million dollars, liquid, and held major shares in the bank.

I explained to him what had just transpired, thinking he would want to cover the notes until Leggett got back on his feet. I told him the law office was a little short due to all the hullabaloo, and just kind of waited for him to offer to help out. Instead, he told me how disappointed he was, and that he felt his son was getting what he had coming to him.

I couldn't believe it. Leggett had done thousands of dollars worth of legal work for the old guy for nothing and was always looking out for him. Besides which, he was a bigger drunk than Leggett ever was. As I hung up the phone and rocked back in my chair, I thought maybe I was beginning to understand why Leggett was so disenchanted.

About a week and a half after I talked to the treatment center, the bank, and Leggett's father, I was driving down Main Street toward the south end of town where the steak house was located. I passed a lone figure walking on the roadside with his hands in his pockets. I drove by, preoccupied with the errand I was running, then slammed on the brakes. It was Leggett. He had lasted eight days at the Rapid City treatment facility.

Leggett never did come back to work. A few weeks later the bank called, and, hinting they were willing to make a deal, asked if I wanted to buy his shares of the business corporation, his house, or his car. It was tempting in the way such offers are, but even considering it mostly made me feel ghoulish. I offered instead to wind things up if the bank would zero out my share of debt. The bank said they thought I had given all I had to give to the situation and accepted my offer.

I decided it was time to move on for a number of reasons, and I visited with people I had come to know in Brookings before I left. One of them was Jack Marken who had originally hired me at South Dakota State as a teaching assistant. As I got ready to go, he said, "You know, practicing law always seemed to me to go against everything you stand for."

Leggett helped me move to Grand Forks, North Dakota. We took a week to do it, drinking beer, telling stories, and whooping it up like we had in the old days. We didn't talk about what had happened, although it would affect us for years. Leggett laughed like hell when I drove to the campus of the University of North Dakota and told him I was going to enroll in the Ph.D. program in literature.

When I left Brookings, I knew I would never go back. In fact, I was already planning to go to the University of Arizona to study Indian literature, but time had run out to make such a move that fall. The University of North Dakota was handy, and it was the closest place that had a Ph.D. program, so I went there for the winter.

That fall was also the end of another major part of my life. After nearly eighteen years of marriage, I took another woman to Grand Forks to live with me. My wife and I had been a couple since she was thirteen and I was fifteen. We had grown up together, surviving by our wits and the generosity of my family. We had three children together and by 1987, when we divorced, the oldest was married and on her own.

During the time we were in Minneapolis, my wife worked for a legal clinic called D*I*A*L L*A*W*Y*E*R*S. She was very good with numbers and in two or three years time worked her way into a position of responsibility and respect. I, on the other hand, was still running on the edge of the rainbow.

She moved back to Brookings with me, and for awhile it looked as if we might have some breathing room again, like we had for a time in law school. That, however, was not to be. When things began to unravel for Leggett and me, and I realized I was on my way back to square one, I made some hard decisions.

First, I decided to get out of law and devote myself to writing and the study of literature. Second, I decided to give my wife the option to stop being tossed about in the wake of my ever-changing plans. I moved out, and after only a short protest she moved back to Minneapolis, resumed her career at the legal clinic, and is now living what she calls a less challenging but very satisfying life.

We had struggled so hard for so long, and had been foiled so many times by what was beginning to appear to me to be an insurmountable accident of birth at the bottom of the totem pole, that I think we were both just ready to try something else.

The next spring I left Grand Forks just as soon as I could and headed for Tucson. Chuck Woodard at South Dakota State had turned me on to Arizona, where Larry Evers, Scott Momaday, and Joy Harjo were all on staff at the university. Leslie Silko had also made Tucson her headquarters, although she had withdrawn from teaching.

I went to Grand Forks with Sandi, a woman I had met in Brookings, but when I left for Tucson she stayed there and I went south alone. We were both recently divorced and had come to the realization we were still on the rebound, which seemed to mean we were still living out things from our previous lives.

One sign was how we adopted a kind of gospel tune mentality and "loved to tell the story." Another was how when courtship drew to a close, and we began to encounter our own problems, we kept proclaiming we had already "been there, done that," and, by God, we weren't going through the same problems again. We finally wished each other a happy life and went our separate ways.

It was the first time I had ever been alone in my life, and it was at the same time one of the most difficult things I had ever experienced and the best thing I ever did for myself. Except for having my kids at Christmas and during summers, I remained alone the three years I was at Arizona.

My children—Lorna, Peter, and Sydney—have handled this complex situation admirably, and for that I am very grateful. They are all doing well and have reinforced something I read once—that children can be incredibly understanding and supportive if given the chance.

My children and I have developed a set of rituals that include traveling, eating, watching movies, and much talking. We value our time together because it is limited, but that doesn't mean we restrict ourselves to niceties.

One night as we were preparing to go see the movie *Batman,* I walked into the living room to see if everybody was ready. Before I had a chance to say anything, my daughter interjected flatly.

"Dad, no."

"What do you mean, 'no?'" I asked.

"No," she said again, rolling her eyes at Peter.

I looked at Peter standing across the room with his arms folded. "No, Dad," he repeated.

"What do you mean?" I looked at both of them then, baffled.

"Dad, I'm going to try to tell you this nicely," Peter continued. "You're not going to the movie wearing those clothes."

"That's right, Dad," Sydney said, taking my hand and leading me toward the closet.

I couldn't believe it. They made me change what I thought were perfectly acceptable clothes, then lectured me about it on the way to the movie. I thought my old knee-length khaki shorts with the red Pistachio stain on the right leg, black socks, and comfortable, though worn, tennis shoes were fine.

Leaving the law, my wife, and my family so far behind was an awful chance to take, but it turned out to be the thing I needed to do to finally find my place. One way this happened was I discovered certain individuals at the university who were more informative and supportive than I could have ever hoped for.

The most helpful of these individuals was Larry Evers, professor of Native American literature, who was also graduate student supervisor in the English department while I was there. Like Charles Woodard at South Dakota State, Dr. Evers made the kind of commitment to my program without which graduate students do not succeed at this kind of endeavor. Unfortunately, such individuals are rare.

Anyway, Evers pointed me to the work I needed to do, and I discovered that my own writing was the way I needed to do it. The work was difficult, and the inanity of dealing with a large university bureaucracy was downright frightening at times, but I found I was able to commit myself in a way I had never been able to before. It is hard to express what that means to someone who has felt out of step for most of a lifetime.

I was getting close to finishing my degree when my mother called one day and left a message on my machine that my Aunt Sis had died that morning. I went home for the funeral and realized for the first time how much things had changed in my life. My grandmother's houses had disappeared. There were no cattle anymore, or horses. Only five of us were left who remembered the way things used to be. I had been gone from Montana for eleven years and only remotely resembled the person I was when I left.

My aunt had a huge funeral, and I realized she had come to be respected as an elder by the entire Fort Belknap community. Although my family as I used to know it was nearly gone, it had expanded through marriage to twice its original size. I laughed to myself as I observed how we were now mingled with the children of people my aunt would have shot on sight thirty years ago.

After the funeral I returned to Arizona, finished my coursework, and took a job in northern Idaho. I was delighted to have a job and to be closer to home, and I looked forward to being able to visit with family and friends more often. Adjusting to the move was chaotic, however, and I didn't have much of a chance to think about such things until Neil called late in the fall and said my uncle had died.

I went home again, and this time my family told me they wanted me to give the eulogy at the funeral. It was a request I didn't expect, and an honor. It also literally ended my young man days in the way that Grovons have of doing such things. It is not uncommon for Indians to avoid such responsibilities of adulthood for remarkable periods of time, and I had avoided them about as long as anybody I knew. I was forty-four years old. I gave the eulogy, an experience I remember vividly nearly a year later.

> "Buck Cole has always been an important part of my life in many ways. I remember Sis telling him once he should get after me for something and his replying that he might as well go get the axe and hit me in the head with it—and it was true, I never could bear his disapproval in any way. So I did what he wanted me to . . . most of the time . . . and that has stood me in good stead throughout my life.
>
> "I know Neil, Wink, Skip, and Michelle all had their own relationships with him, too, and I think he had a way of making each one of us feel we were special to him, each

in our own way. None of us lacked energy or self-confidence and we were each one of us a handful at one time or another. We were no match for Buck, however, and especially not for him and Sis together. They played us like guitars, one of them giving us what-for while the other remained silent, indicating things would blow over with the other one if we straightened up. Then they would change roles the next time—I think they kind of took turns fronting for each other in the business of raising kids.

"As time passed and we all had our own families, Buck shined his light on them, too. Being a daughter-in-law in our family wasn't an easy thing to do, given how clannish we were, but Buck always made sure the necessary doors were opened and our families soon became his, too. He loved children as much as anyone I've ever seen, and he thoroughly enjoyed every one of them he could get his hands on. A couple of years ago, when he was pretty well confined to his chair, I watched him lure one of my grandkids over to him with his candy dish, where she stayed the rest of the day. He had a horse that had been wire cut as a colt and got to be kind of a pet, and he gave that horse to kids from Seattle, Washington, to Southam, North Dakota. He gave that horse away so many times it's a wonder it could still stand. And every kid he gave that horse to believed it was really his or hers.

"There were many other people in Buck's life besides family. One of the earliest memories I have is Buck and Benny Stevens's friendship and how Benny wanted Buck with him when he died. There were many others—and I

*won't try to mention all of them for fear of leaving some-
one out—but they had fun together fishing, traveling,
working, and just plain visiting in the best tradition of
friendship.*

*"Buck Cole was a good cowboy and a good business-
man in a place and time where that wasn't easy to do. He
also was a cultural intermediary between the Indian and
white communities, and that is very important in a world
that needs so badly to be able to live together. Buck was a
good friend, father, uncle, grandfather, and eventually a respected elder to all of us his family grew to include. As I
have traveled around the country and have observed the
alienation and loneliness that is so widespread among individuals, families, and communities, I have come to appreci-
ate what we all had with Buck Cole, and it is for that
reason that I hate most to see him go.*

*"I want him to have peace, however, and rest, and to
pass on these words from an education he supported me
through as it went on, and on, and on . . .*

> *Death be not proud, though some have called thee
> Mighty and dreadfull, for, thou are not soe.
> For, those, whom thou think'st, thou dost overthrow,
> Die not, poore death, . . .
> One short sleepe past, wee wake eternally,
> And death shall be no more; Death, thou shalt die."*

In the time that has passed since the deaths of my grandfather,
grandmother, aunt, and uncle, I notice that, in the way I always
measure distance by how far places are from the ranch, I have be-

gun to measure time by the passing of my people. After a long time I have returned to the Northwest only to find that most of them are gone. But, to my surprise, others who represent a kind of renewal have come along, and that seems as it should be.

In the same way, most of my wounds have healed. I still smolder on some accounts, but even those now seem to be more of a resource than a liability. I am even ready to come out of the closet in the way of people of this time and announce that I am a grandfather, not once, but three times, with number four on the way. What a long, strange trip it has been, and, in the words I once wrote to Dick Hugo,

> I was surprised when I returned. Not
> that you were dead but that Tuesdays
> could break hard work down to simple
> gestures. I imagine growing civilized
> and remember your forward Buick fondly. It
> was cars we had in common, and the need
> for reassuring distance in a rear-view mirror.
> Winter won't leave us alone. Missoula was
> better to you, and the pulp-belt bars
> gave you reflections in a romantic eye.
> I read the pattern of waves in my blood,
> know enough to sit tight next to the Red River
> until silent highways tap a better message.
>
> It has been a long time. Remember that
> bar down by the mill? Lives cheaper
> than beer and the wrong look could tip
> the scales all the way to China. You

got out of there just in time. Or maybe
you would have preferred to go for it
with Bogus Red. He squared things once
and for all and is now talking accounts
to his dick and a succession of visitors
who never show at the crowbar hotel.
Missoula was okay but I didn't ask for
much more than a quick goodbye.

What can I say? I don't drink much
anymore. Days go diachronic. Little
Mayans watch our buildings from far away
with knowing eyes. Some guy from Tacoma came
inland looking to fulfill the need of his life.
He read the signs, then immediately reduced
murder to love. Another grand parable of sin,
grace, redemption. Other lovers caught up
with him in Florida and killed him back.
I can't talk about the fish just now
but they do seem to think that communication
as we know it is about to change big time.

P.S. Yellowstone burned down last summer.

Nanahax wu

The time of wisdom in Gros Ventre life

In 1992 I became assistant professor of English at Lewis-Clark State College, Lewiston, Idaho. Lewis-Clark is an as-of-yet largely undiscovered gem comprised of some of the best American education has to offer without many of the negative aspects of larger institutions. The faculty is first-rate, the instructor-student ratio very reasonable, and most politics are left to sister schools. Remarkably, the faculty, the deans of the various divisions, and even the academic vice-president all teach.

I still don't do this for the money. Salaries at Lewis-Clark, similar to most colleges across the country, continue to send the wrong message about what is important; they inspire more people to sell real estate than to teach literature, and they jeopardize democracy by weakening faith in the economic system.

What I do it for is the opportunity to live and work in an academic community and to devote myself to writing and the study of literature. My current duties include teaching basic English classes at the nearby Nez Perce Indian Reservation; teaching composition, introduction to literature, and American Indian literature on campus, and serving as director of American Indian Studies.

Although I am no longer a student, I continue to study American Indian literature, submitting papers to scholarly journals instead of college professors for review. This work has met with some success, which pleases me because I feel strongly it is important for someone with firsthand knowledge of existing Indian communities to play a part in the interpretation of Indian texts.

My analysis of these texts is essentially informed by my life, as well as by my academic training, a phenomenon I think enhances interpretation considerably, bringing to bear the experience of having "walked the walk" as well as having learned to "talk the talk." In many ways this method of analysis derives from having "progressed" in measurable modern ways but also having left behind much that was necessary to be ultimately successful. Because I allowed myself to become an outsider to family, landscape, and tribal identity, I was, after a while, poorly equipped to cope with challenges that arose. Finally, I began to learn that I must start over in certain ways.

Until I began to learn how to deal with success that distanced me from family and community, and the law firm star system which reinforced the idea I was "different," my success only led to a kind of paralysis.

I was fortunate enough to have some athletic ability and competed a little around Montana. I also practiced law for a time, and these experiences helped propel me to wonderful and lonely places. I don't play ball anymore, on the court or in court. Like the beer I drank at night after playing, these things became a drug. If there was a stronger connection between them and real energy sources of family, landscape, and education, there would be nothing wrong with them. But right now there is not that strong connection, and athletic and legal games too easily became just another escape from reality.

American Indian texts seem to me to be almost the modern equivalent of medicine bundles of old. I have been drawn to their power to contain and reflect history and culture as well as to enter into a dialogue with the audiences they reach. These texts, in my opinion, are one of the moving forces of Indian culture today. They do more to inform and teach both Indians and Others about themselves, about one another, and about more effective ways of living than anything else I am aware of.

I am very interested in being a part of the writing community as a way of contributing to the universe and "making something of myself." I believe in writing oneself and the world, not as something better or worse than, say, the practice of law, but as a way of playing a more active role in the process of inventing self.

The autobiographical form of this book is a step toward achieving that goal. I was born with pierced ears, something Grovons believe signifies the rebirth of a very old Indian. Because of this, I believe there are traces of many things at work in my life as well as the things I can instantly comprehend, and that is confusing at times.

As a result, at a certain point it was necessary for me to reorder my life. When I left Fort Belknap, the features of its familiar landscape no longer centered me, and I became centered upon myself. In doing so, I got lost. I failed to mark the trail of my journey, and when I arrived at my outbound destination I had no means of ordering it.

Implicit in this is that being able to find the way out, the way back, and being able to mark the way as a person's life journey progresses is a model that corresponds to awareness of the past, present, and future. Once I realized the importance of such awareness, I began to imagine what I needed to find my way again.

In order to do this, I needed to "start over" symbolically. My original beginning, a journey complicated by my background, needed to be retraced and marked properly, beginning with the important guidepost of my parentage. I needed to understand my own illegitimacy, and the Fort Belknap community's reaction— that to a certain degree they imagined it as foreign contamination of Gros Ventre blood, and how that contributed to my own feelings of alienation.

I needed to go back before I could go forward, and mark the intersections created by my heritage, my family, my education, and my father. Once these intersections were marked, they could be imagined as a part of natural change rather than as elements of destruction. Establishing these points of reference then enabled me to impose the symbolic order of words on the topography of my journey.

Nanahax wu

After working out this order, it seemed as though some kind of assessment should take place. In making that assessment I discovered what I thought to be some interesting things. For example, I found my thinking about my father had changed somewhat. Although I still believe there are disadvantages to not having a father, there is also a kind of freedom that goes with illegitimacy. Part of a father's legacy to his children is the expectation they will be like him. In the absence of that influence a child has much less obligation to follow in anyone's footsteps and is much more free to evolve a distinctive personality. Something I feel I have been freed to do along these lines is to try a number of different roles along the way to settling on the one I feel is best for me.

Similarly, living in both white and Indian worlds allowed me to pick and choose among those cultures to a certain degree. Although I have always identified more strongly with my Fort Belknap background than with my white experiences, I have also happily adopted a Euro-centric academic lifestyle as well.

On the other hand, although I am very pleased by the progress I have made in certain areas, I feel I have not always fared so well with family relationships. I am the only academic in my extended family, and although I think I am somewhat of a curiosity to them, I also suffer at times by being labeled somewhat of a bon vivant, rather than as a "hard worker," the way they see themselves.

In moments of indignation I have asserted that my critics are probably incapable of moving furniture the number of times required to achieve a Ph.D., let alone do the course work. I am afraid, however, having lived in a number of different places mostly translates to instability to those I seek to convince.

As if being labeled less than hard working is not bad enough, there are times when I am myself tempted to believe I am self-indulgent. At times when I have been hunched over in front of the word processor for days, or when I am searching library stacks for more books, I sometimes feel I am in danger of becoming a huge head with no body at all.

I also keep thinking that all I need to do to get back in shape is not to join Gold's Gym, but instead to get a few cows. I won't try to understand 'em, just rope, throw, and brand 'em. In reality, while other people might do such things, or buy Nordic Track machines, I often move all my boxes of books to yet another rented hovel.

Between the sister cities of Lewiston, Idaho, and Clarkston, Washington, the Snake River joins the Clearwater River in a confluence protected by canyon walls nearly 2,500 feet high. The United States Army Corps of Engineers has constructed paved walking paths on top of the dike that protects Lewiston from the river.

The dike is a great place to walk, and to contemplate things that might be of importance, or not. The depth of the valley protects it from severe weather and the river lends drama at any time of day. It is like being in a cave, or belly, with a river leading out that could take you all the way to the sea.

I do my roadwork there, thrashing out whatever is going on at the time or enjoying the day as I make the three miles from Lewiston Grain Growers to the information center and back. I was not taught to reason, negotiate, mediate, in times of stress—I was taught to fight like a Badger out of its hole. Nowadays I fight with this pavement, stomping it, grinding it under my feet, running over it with the speed of flight.

Yesterday I stepped lightly, turning my morning literature class over and over in my mind like a shiny object. It is close to the end of the semester, and I have set this class up since day one for the short story we discussed this morning.

The story is entitled "A Father's Story," and was written by a man named Andre Dubus. It is about a man who is divorced, and lonely. He has a child, a daughter to whom he has remained connected. His daughter kills a person with her car one night and the father protects her from the consequences by not reporting the accident to the police.

My students always bite on the moral dilemma faced by the father in his decision to protect his daughter. There are usually older students in the class who have grown or nearly grown children of their own, and that adds just the right mix of perspective to the views of younger students.

Invariably, the class splits nearly down the middle when asked if they would turn their own children over to the authorities under similar circumstances. The resulting discussion is lively and almost always allows me to climb up on one of my last soapboxes of the semester.

This last soapbox allows me to deliver my views with regard to family. Usually, a student will ask me what I would do if one of my children were involved in such an accident. I say I would not call the police, that I would do exactly as the father did in the story.

Then I say that, based on my experiences as doctor, lawyer, and Indian chief, that I believe family provides the best return on time and resources of anything I am aware of. Then, picking up speed, I go on to say that, in addition, I also believe any influence that takes the individual away from his or her place of origin on any kind of permanent basis is wrongheaded.

Usually, before I can really get rolling on the virtues of sharing versus hoarding, or decry monolithic capitalism, the bell rings. For some time now, small dragon that this is to slay, I have been quite happy with it.

In the American Indian Lives Series